D0021117

# Experiencing Erickson

*An Introduction to the Man and His Work*

# Experiencing Erickson

## *An Introduction to the Man and His Work*

by

Jeffrey K. Zeig, Ph.D.

with
Transcript of Milton H. Erickson, M.D.

BRUNNER/MAZEL, *Publishers* • New York

**Library of Congress Cataloging-in-Publication Data**

Zeig, Jeffrey K., 1947-
  Experiencing Erickson.

  Bibliography: p. 183
  1. Erickson, Milton H. 2. Psychiatrists—United
States—Biography. 3. Hypnotism—Therapeutic use.
4. Psychotherapy, Brief. I. Erickson, Milton H.
II. Title.
RC33952.E73Z45 1985      616.89′0092′4      85-19457
ISBN 0-87630-409-9

*Published by*
BRUNNER/MAZEL, INC.
19 Union Square West
New York, New York 10003

MANUFACTURED IN THE UNITED STATES OF AMERICA

# Foreword

"Ericksonian Psychotherapy" is the name given to a body of techniques most of which have been taken from the lectures, seminars, workshops, and writings of Milton H. Erickson, M.D., perhaps the foremost practitioner of hypnosis in the United States. More important than the actual techniques is the philosophy behind the methods as well as the tactical interpersonal approaches to the patient that are designed to liberate potentials for self-help in either the hypnotic or waking state (Erickson & Rossi, 1980; Haley, 1973). Discounting the myths and anecdotes about Erickson that so commonly emanate from devotees and detractors of any charismatic figure, "Ericksonian Psychotherapy" has had a significant influence on thousands of professionals and is registering an imprint on American psychotherapy itself. This is evidenced by the many papers and volumes about Erickson that have been and continue to be published (Hammond, 1984; Rossi & Ryan, 1985; Rossi et al., 1983; Zeig, 1980, 1982, 1985a, 1985b).

The present volume, largely a personal account of the author's experiences with Erickson, is an important contribution toward understanding many of the attitudes and methods utilized by Erickson with his patients. Some of his interventions were an outcome of coping techniques he employed to moderate the pain and disabilities resulting from his childhood poliomyelitis. Struggles with his handicaps made for a unique blend of resourcefulness, flexibility, ingenuity, artfulness, and improvisation which, blended with an unorthodox style and a penchant for brinksmanship, have created a model of psychotherapy that is exciting to read about, but difficult to duplicate by the average therapist schooled in the traditional designs of treatment. There are, nevertheless, lessons to be learned not only from the dexterous ways Erickson related to himself and to his patients, but also from the dramatic expediences devised by this talented innovator.

Acting variantly with each patient as counselor, analyst, referee, arbiter, advocate, prompter, mentor, accepting authority, or punitive parent, Erickson stressed the uniqueness of each individual, who, motivated by singular needs and idiosyncratic defenses, required original modes of approach rather than orthodox, unimaginative, and doctrinal styles. He considered himself and his words, intonations, manner of speaking, and bodily movements vehicles of influence that could promote change. Interested in action rather than theory, he considered traditional theory a handicap that anchored therapists to a bedrock of hopeless imponderables. Toward this end, he suggested, cajoled, and maneuvered with a host of individual multilevel communicative thrusts, verbal and nonverbal, that were fabricated to influence the patient without the latter's full awareness of being manipulated. Sometimes he failed, but this merely provided him with new incentives to overcome the patient's reluctance to utilize latent resources and potentials for change.

Frequently Erickson would join the manifest resistance and seemingly side with the patient's illness and defenses, or he would assign the patient to what appeared to be peculiar, irrelevant tasks. He would offer homespun advice and commonsense remedies that made use of the obvious. Conversely, he would utilize metaphors and obtuse inferences that were not exactly to the point. He would set up situations "where people would spontaneously realize their previously unrecognized abilities to change" (Zeig, 1985b). But there was a design in these contrivances if no more than to confuse patients enough to force them to open their minds to a different way of looking at things. Techniques were not selected in advance but were tailored to the exigencies of the immediate situation. Even though Erickson refused to identify himself with any of the well-known schools of psychotherapy, he often utilized behavioral, cognitive, analytic, and other methodologies within the framework of his unique modes of operation. Hypnosis was employed when it was considered useful in expediting therapy. His immediate objective was symptom relief and problem-solving, although personality and value change were considered ideal goals that might sooner or later be achieved.

Among psychotherapists there are some who worship Erickson with a reverance that borders on idolatry. Every word, sentiment, opinion, or act is presumed to have an inspired meaning. Such deification, rooted in expectations of timeless power and omnipotence, can ultimately lead to disillusionment. Equally prejudiced are those who regard Erickson as a maverick whose egregious methods are a passing fancy that will eventually be consigned to the dustbin of outmoded schemes. These attitudes do injustice to a highly creative, imaginative, and original mind which evolved novel approaches to some of the most baffling problems in psychotherapy. Erickson was a marvelous influencing machine crafted by years of struggle mastering his painful physical disability. His courage, sensitivity, perceptiveness, and unique modes of coping made him, in the words of Haley (1973), an "uncommon therapist." But his approaches, blending with his "uncommon" personality and styles of operation, may not be so easily transposed, digested, and utilized by others.

A poignant criticism of Erickson's strategic therapy is that it is overvalued by those who believe that clever tactics can substitute for disciplined training. Technical modes of operation are only a fragment of what goes into the gestalt of a psychotherapeutic program. For one thing, we must know how to deal with a host of variables related to patients' defenses, belief systems, and characterologic peculiarities that can negate and cancel out the effect of all of our strategic interventions.

Erickson was an expert in the utilization of ploys to bypass resistances, having in his upbringing sharpened his wits on the grindstone of stubborn, virtually impossible physical obstacles. I remember one instance when, on a trip to New York, Erickson came to visit me at the exact time that a patient arrived for his session. The patient was a young obsessive-compulsive who was making his own life and the existence of others around him miserable with offensive behavior and obtrusive thoughts of disease, death, and destruction. Since early childhood he had been under the care of an impressive succession of psychoanalysts, behavior therapists, and hypnotists whom he gradually wore down with his constant complaints of being damaged rather than helped by their ministrations. He was finally referred to me for hypnosis since none of the other professionals who used hypnosis could succeed in getting him into a trance. I, too, failed miserably and after several months of futile sessions I looked forward to the day when I could refer him to someone else and peacefully join the long line of frustrated professionals who had given up trying to help.

It was by some fortunate stroke of providence that Erickson walked in on the start of another unhappy session. "Milton," I queried jokingly, "do you believe you can hypnotize this young man?" Erickson loved challenges and he could not let this one go by, especially since the patient appeared negative to any more attempts to get him into a trance. In a short time Erickson convinced the patient to accompany him to an adjoining room where he kept him for almost three hours. Periodically, I peered into the room to find what I had expected, namely that the patient was a potent adversary, completely awake and grinning at Erickson's failure to do very much with him. But Erickson never gave up and after two hours, to my astonishment and, I am sure, to that of the patient, Erickson succeeded in inducing a somnambulistic trance during which the patient hallucinated objects and animals at suggestion. I was as much impressed by Erickson's persistence in the face of failure as I was by his induction skills.

Following this demonstration, I had a mighty sick boy on my hands who, probably because he had yielded control for the first time, went into a state of great anxiety, to the alarm of his parents. But this situation presented me with an opportunity to establish meaningful contact and to work through aspects of his death fear, enabling him to achieve considerable relief from symptoms. I cite this case as an example of Erickson's great capacity to tune into and and to resolve resistances to his ministrations.

Other variables relate to a patient's special talents or ineptitudes to utilize techniques that are prescribed, and here Erickson showed an uncanny capacity to accelerate the patient's learning. Many therapists fail to recognize that a goodly number of patients can respond idiosyncratically to some interventions which, though executed with care, may produce paradoxical effects. Working with this dimension may constitute the principal therapeutic task for a considerable stretch of time. Erickson's unique genius rested in his ability to discern with extraordinary facility not only the areas of malfunction that required correction, but also the blocks within the patient that prevented his getting well. He would then fashion interventions to remove these interferences with astonishing rapidity. Jeffrey Zeig provides here many illustrations of how Erickson went about doing this. Accordingly, this book constitutes a valuable addition to the growing literature about one of the most interesting personalities in our field.

*Lewis R. Wolberg, M.D.*
*Founder and Emeritus Dean*
*Postgraduate Center for Mental Health*
*New York City*

## REFERENCES

Erickson, M.H., & Rossi, E. (Eds.). (1980). *Innovative Hypnotherapy. Collected Papers of Milton H. Erickson on Hypnosis.* New York: Irvington.

Haley, J. (1973). *Uncommon Therapy: The Psychiatric Techniques of Milton H. Erickson, M.D.* New York: W. W. Norton.

Hammond, D.C. (1984). Myths about Erickson and Ericksonian hypnosis. *American Journal of Clinical Hypnosis, 26,* 236-245.

Rossi, E., & Ryan, M. (Eds.). (1985). *Life Reframing in Hypnosis: The Seminars, Workshops and Lectures of Milton H. Erickson, Vol. II.* New York: Irvington.

Rossi, E., Ryan, M., & Sharp, F. (Eds.). (1983). *Healing in Hypnosis: The Seminars, Workshops and Lectures of Milton H. Erickson, Vol. I.* New York: Irvington.

Zeig, J.K. (Ed.). (1980). *A Teaching Seminar With Milton H. Erickson.* New York: Brunner/Mazel.

Zeig, J.K. (Ed.). (1982). *Ericksonian Approaches to Hypnosis and Psychotherapy.* New York: Brunner/Mazel.

Zeig, J.K. (Ed.). (1985a). *Ericksonian Psychotherapy, Vol. I.* New York: Brunner/Mazel.

Zeig, J.K. (Ed.). (1985b). *Experiencing Erickson.* New York: Brunner/Mazel.

# Contents

# Introduction

This book presents an orientation to the Hypnotic Psychotherapy of Milton H. Erickson, M.D. It consists of three essays and a transcript of a dialogue with Erickson in 1973. The volume is a subjective statement and personal account; it is not meant to be an objective or critical evaluation. I am not in a position to be critical and it is difficult to be objective about Erickson; he was a man who engendered strong responses. Before delving into Erickson's style I think it may be helpful to understand some basic aspects of Ericksonian methods.

Ericksonian psychotherapy is a pragmatic, structural approach based on ascertaining and modifying existing maladaptive patterns; promoting change takes precedence over clarifying the past, or insight into the meaning or function of symptoms. To promote patient-based change, the therapist meets the patient at his or her frame of reference, and multilevel therapeutic communication is individualized in order to identify, elicit, develop, recombine, and utilize patient resources. While therapeutic techniques are drawn from powerful hypnotic methods, formal hypnosis is not always used. Naturalistic techniques (hypnotherapy without a formal trance induction procedure) are used because they are generally more effective.

Flexibility in approach is emphasized; there is no preconceived set for the number of required sessions. However, treatment tends to be brief and problem-oriented. If possible, even the length of the session is determined by the task to be accomplished, not by the position of the hour hand on the clock.

Commonly, goals are determined by the therapist who often presents commonsense understandings and advice in such a way that patients can respond therapeutically. Usually this necessitates the use of indirect techniques.

As will be seen, indirect techniques consist of communicating one-step removed. Often this entails "parallel communication." Rather than addressing problems and solutions directly, the therapist presents a parallel through the use of such techniques as dramatic anecdotes and analogies. Also, the therapist can formulate advice and present it one-step removed through the use of binds and therapeutic implication. Through the use of indirection, less resistance is engendered and the patient energizes the therapy, responding with or without conscious awareness.

Rather than elucidating technical aspects of Erickson's methods, this book presents Erickson's style and orientation to psychotherapy. This is in keeping with Erickson's own philosophy: In teaching he deemphasized technique and theory, believing both to be limiting. Psychotherapists who try to validate a particular theory, or who look to use a specific technique, will find a way to accomplish their goal even if it requires whittling the corners of the patient's psyche to fit the therapist's preconceived theory or method. I believe it was Mark Twain who noted, if you want to use a hammer, an awful lot of things will look like nails.

As will be seen, Erickson taught an orientation. Jay Haley (1982), one of Erickson's main proponents, noted that if he could really understand Erickson's orientation, new therapeutic vistas would become apparent. This volume is intended to provide new vistas for understanding how therapists can help patients live more effectively.

It is written with the novice therapist in mind. Much of the reported experiences with Erickson occurred when I was a novice therapist, and one can see how Erickson approached the task of training a beginning practitioner. However, Erickson's deceptive simplicity should be enough to intrigue even the most accomplished practitioner.

When either the novice or experienced therapist initially encounters Erickson, there are three discounts that frequently surface: 1) the idea of manipulation; 2) the difficulty of applying Erickson's method is one's own therapeutic work; and 3) Erickson as a cult figure. Each one of these will be addressed separately.

"Manipulation" has a negative connotation. However, as communication analysts such as Watzlawick point out, it is impossible not to manipulate. Interpersonal exchange is predicated on manipulation. Manipulation is unavoidable; the issue is how to manipulate constructively and therapeutically.

One difficulty in integrating Erickson's approach into one's own personal work is that it takes considerable effort. Erickson was quite disciplined in his methods, and he worked to develop himself as an effective communicator. His therapies could be analyzed in closer scrutiny than any other practitioner. Verbal and nonverbal maneuvers were carefully designed to elicit maximum therapeutic responses. His effectiveness was grounded in his developed perceptiveness of nuance. He trained himself to pick up the minimal clues that depict a patient's strengths—strengths that can be used to solve problems. In some ways he approached his cases like a great detective. Once Erickson's solution is presented, it becomes clear that the important clues were always apparent to one who cared to attend and use common sense.

As far as cults are concerned, students of psychotherapy have searched for a true "father magician" who can personify the best human values to which psychotherapy aspires. In many ways, Milton Erickson fit the bill; he consistently struggled to bring out the best in himself and those around him. There is an attraction as well as a repulsion to strong figures. Often, psychotherapeutic movements have centered around a dynamic personality. Sometimes detractors have attached the pejorative label of "cult" to such movements.

This label can serve as a convenient way to dismiss important work without providing thoughtful evaluation. "Cults" are automatically considered to be always mindless and myopic—to be avoided at all costs.

Traditionally, psychotherapy has been a breeding ground for sectarian movements. Starting with Freud, the legends of psychotherapy have been deified and movements have been formed around their personality and theory.

Erickson did not present himself as a leader of a cult or movement. He was a highly unique person who promoted individuality in himself and others. He had no desire to establish even a school of psychotherapy.

It will be evident how much I revered Erickson. He was an impressive innovator who discreetly departed from tradition, and had new things to say about psychotherapy. Many outstanding professionals were impressed by Erickson and sought him out for collaboration both personally and professionally, including Margaret Mead, Gregory Bateson, Jay Haley, John Weakland, Ernest Rossi, Stephen Lankton, and Joseph Barber.

In contrast to *A Teaching Seminar with Milton H. Erickson* (1980) where I presented how Erickson taught a group of students, this book shows how Erickson worked with me as an individual. In it I describe my personal reactions. This is an insider's view of Milton Erickson. Many people have tried to present Erickson in an objective light; most try to keep the personality of the author out of the work. That is not my goal.

Because much of this volume is about the one-to-one interaction Erickson had with me, it is of a personal nature. Because this book is personally revealing, I hope it will provide therapists a chance to personally identify as well as professionally learn.

There are a number of people I wish to thank. My Editor, Deborah Laake, and my Administrative Assistant, Barbara Bellamy, were instrumental in the process of writing this book. I am also grateful to Mrs. Elizabeth Erickson, Sherron S. Peters, Kristina K. Erickson, Stephen Lankton, John Moran, Larry Gindhart, and Michael Yapko who read sections and provided important feedback that was incorporated into the manuscript.

*Phoenix, AZ*                                                                    *Jeffrey K. Zeig*
*August, 1985*

# Experiencing Erickson

*An Introduction to the
Man and His Work*

# CHAPTER 1

# Erickson's Creativity

"Genius" refers to the attendant spirit of a person. It also signifies a person endowed with transcendent mental ability and inventiveness. Erickson's genius derived from the intersection of his intelligence, humanity, inquisitiveness, inventiveness, and perceptiveness. He also was diligent in developing and honing his abilities.

Erickson's genius was in four areas: as a hypnotist; as a psychotherapist; as a teacher; and as an individual who turned physical disability to advantage. Considered together, his achievements in these four areas make him seem like a person who was larger than life.

## THE HYPNOTIST

If one were studying the history of hypnosis, one would probably read first about the 18th century practitioner Mesmer. And then about

Charcot, Braid, Liébeault, and Bernheim, all of whom worked with hypnosis in the 19th century.

And then, in the 20th century, one would read about Erickson. He was the father of modern medical hypnosis. His creativity in devising new methods of hypnotic induction and utilization was extraordinary. He co-authored five books on the topic and published more than 130 professional articles, most of them on hypnotherapy. He was founder and first president of the American Society of Clinical Hypnosis; he initiated and for ten years edited its official organ, *The American Journal of Clinical Hypnosis*. He traveled widely, especially in the United States, to teach hypnosis to professionals and was generally known as "Mr. Hypnosis" (Secter, 1982, p. 453). Erickson legitimized hypnosis so that it was no longer the "court jester in the solemn halls of orthodoxy" (Watzlawick, 1982, p. 148).

Prior to Erickson, hypnotherapy was not a distinct discipline or primary therapeutic tool. However, hypnosis has been an important seed in the development of disparate disciplines of psychotherapy. The psychoanalyst, Sigmund Freud; the Gestalt therapist, Fritz Perls; the behaviorist, Joseph Wolpe; and the Transactional Analyst, Eric Berne—all were familiar with hypnosis but rejected it in favor of developing their particular approaches to therapy and advancing their theories of personality and change. Erickson stayed with hypnosis because he was a pragmatist who saw that hypnosis could influence a patient to change. He did not develop a special theory of hypnosis, but he departed radically from the traditional use of hypnosis whereby the operator force-feeds suggestions into a passive subject. Instead his method was to bring forth and utilize inner resources (cf. Hammond, 1984).

Ericksonian hypnosis is used to elicit therapeutic *responses*, the essence of which is to get the patient to *cooperate*. Patients enter psychotherapy because they have difficulty accomplishing tasks they set for themselves. It is the job of the therapist to get the patient to follow his or her own desires to the extent possible, and to this end hypnosis can often be effective in surmounting impasses. It makes more available to patients their own potentials for self-help.

Although formal hypnosis is a model par excellence of influence communication, rather than using it solely, Erickson pioneered naturalistic methods, i.e., taking techniques from hypnosis and effectively applying them to psychotherapy without the necessity of an induction ritual. Actually, he used formal hypnosis in only a fifth of the cases he treated (Beahrs, 1971), but he consistently used hypnotic technique even when he was not "doing hypnosis." (The cases of John, Joe, and Barbie were such examples, and will be discussed later.) The naturalistic approach was the essence of Erickson's strategic approach to brief therapy, the second area of Erickson's genius.

## THE PSYCHOTHERAPIST

With the publication by Jay Haley of *Uncommon Therapy* (1973), Erickson became generally known as the father of brief strategic approaches to psychotherapy. As a remarkably successful practitioner of these approaches, he added a tremendous number of new cases and methods to the literature of brief strategic psychotherapy; more cases are still being discovered in tapes from old lectures (e.g., Rossi, Ryan, & Sharp, 1983; Rossi & Ryan, 1985).

Haley (1980) wrote that therapy is a problem, not a solution. The problem is that patients are in therapy. The solution is to get them out of therapy and living their own independent lives as quickly as possible. Erickson would have agreed with that position. His strategic therapy was a common-sense approach, usually directed at the presenting problem. While on the surface his strategic techniques seemed uncommon, actually he had uncommon common sense.

It is a bit bizarre to put a phobic person on a couch and ask him or her to free associate for exactly 50 minutes. It is common sense to get phobic people to violate their phobias by inserting them into the feared situation in such a way that they can learn mastery. In this way and others, Erickson was one of the first modern practitioners to take therapy out of the realm of the patients' mind (and the consulting room) and make it part of their real life. His facility for doing so was an aspect of his great inventiveness and creativity.

## THE TEACHER

Another departure from tradition was Erickson's method of teaching. In 1980, I published *A Teaching Seminar with Milton H. Erickson*

(1980a), a transcript of a one-week seminar for professionals that demonstrated his uncommon teaching methods. He told interesting stories, mainly about successful psychotherapy but also about his family, and he conducted demonstrations of hypnotherapy. He didn't supervise students by listening to tapes of their sessions or by observing them and guiding therapies they conducted. (I was Erickson's student over a six-year time span and he referred many patients to me, but he never saw or heard me conduct a hypnotic induction or a session of therapy.) Instead, Erickson taught by using multiple-level influence communication to elicit resources; this was the same way he did psychotherapy, as well as the same way he did hypnosis. He blurred the lines between "hypnosis," "teaching," and "psychotherapy." When he was teaching, he was doing hypnosis; when he was conducting hypnosis, he was doing psychotherapy.

Erickson was a consistent man whose goal was to communicate as relevantly as possible most of the time; he communicated to have the maximum specified effect. And he always had a goal in mind. An anecdote sheds light on his teaching philosophy. In response to my comment that a tape of one of his old lectures in the 1950s seemed to me like one long hypnotic induction, he said that he didn't listen to his tapes: "I usually didn't teach content; I taught to motivate."

In the Ericksonian concept, there should not be a large distinction between hypnosis, teaching, and psychotherapy because in all of those areas one relies on unconscious learning. The underlying philosophy is that people already have the resources they need to effect change. Therefore, psychotherapy and hypnosis—and to a large extent even teaching—are processes of eliciting and developing resources and helping the person to combine resources in new, more effective ways.

## THE INDIVIDUAL

As original as Erickson was as a hypnotist, psychotherapist, and teacher, he was even more of an original in the way that he lived his life. There were evidences of this every hour, but his individuality was particularly well-expressed in the way he surmounted staggering physical obstacles on his way to a full life.

Erickson's numerous physical problems are recounted below in a letter dated December 10, 1934, from his wife, Elizabeth Erickson to a student who himself had an attack of polio and wrote to her inquiring about Erickson's struggles. Although her account isn't meant as one, Mrs. Erickson's memories are an eloquent testimonial to this fourth area of Erickson's genius, one that eclipsed the previous three.

## About Erickson: His Physical Struggles

My late husband, ·Milton H. Erickson, suffered his initial attack of poliomyelitis at the age of 17 (in 1919). It was an extremely severe infection. He was completely paralyzed, unable to do other than speak and move his eyes and was aware that he was not expected to survive. He was cared for in his farm home by his mother and a live-in practical nurse. As the paralysis subsided to some extent, this nurse, on her own, used the type of therapy later popularized (against much medical opposition) by the Australian nurse, Sister Kenny. That is, she developed a system of hot packs, massage, and moving the paralyzed limbs, and motivating patient participation.

Milton, on his own, developed a system of mental concentration on a minimum movement, mentally reliving such movement over and over. As he regained more strength, he utilized every opportunity to exercise more and more muscles to strengthen them, learning to walk with crutches, learning to balance on and ride his bicycle; and finally, by obtaining a canoe, some basic provisions and camping gear, a few dollars, he planned a summer-long canoe trip, starting at the lake near the University of Wisconsin campus, following the waterway to the Mississippi River and proceeding south beyond St. Louis, returning upriver the same way.

A friend planned on accompanying him but at the last moment withdrew. Milton proceeded alone in spite of his physical handicaps, not telling his parents it would be a trip alone. After many adventures and coping with multiple problems, but learning various means of such coping, and meeting many interesting characters, some of them helpful, he completed the trip in far better health with powerfully developed shoulder muscles, ready to undertake college and medical school.

He told me many years later that his permanent loss of muscles, mostly on the right side, would ordinarily have led to carrying the left shoulder much higher than the right, and a visibly twisted torso. By dint of sheer physical effort, practiced in front of a mirror, he managed to level off his shoulders, greatly increasing the spinal curvature which would have resulted in any case from the polio, but would have been to a much lesser degree. He felt that the more nearly normal appearance was well worth the effort. During World War II, he was given a very intensive physical examination to see if he could be qualified for limited service as a medical officer. X rays taken of his spine at that time were met with amazement and disbelief by the specialists doing the examination.

While he was justifiably proud of this achievement of level shoulders, in retrospect it may have had some long-term bad effects. In his later years, one of his more knowledgeable physicians told me that at least some of his recurrent periods of complete disability, progressive loss of muscles, and great pain might be due to settling of bones of the twisted spinal column aggravated by arthritic changes, leading to pinching and further degeneration of the surviving portions of the spinal nerves.

I first met Milton in 1935 and we were married in 1936. He then was a vigorous, active man, with a marked limp on the right side. He walked with a cane but could do so for long distances. He had broad, powerful shoulders.

He had some brief episodes of pain in muscles and joints, but nothing serious that I can recall until the late 1940s. During the war, the staff duties at Eloise Hospital (later known as Wayne County General Hospital and Infirmary at Eloise) were greatly increased due to lack of personnel. He was also involved in teaching Residents at Eloise, and medical students in the accelerated medical school program at Wayne University College of Medicine in downtown Detroit. Additionally, he spent many hours (either before or after a full day's session at Eloise) giving psychiatric examinations to military inductees at the downtown induction station, riding there and back on the bus as we did not have gasoline. All this work did not bother him.

A point I now wish to make is that his recurrent attacks usually seemed to be triggered by some severe physical stress. In the late summer or early fall of 1947, he was riding his bicycle from our apartment on the grounds to his office (also on the grounds, some distance away). He rode for exercise. A dog ran against the wheel and he was thrown, sustaining scrapes and superficial cuts, some on the face area and with ground-in dirt.

He had never had tetanus toxoid, so decided that no matter the risk (because of his life-long multiple allergies) to take the old style tetanus antitoxin shots. About 10 days later he developed severe serum sickness, including muscle pains, a near-comatose episode, and other symptomatology. He would partly recover, resume his office work and some teaching, then would become ill again.

Finally, in the spring of 1948, he became so ill that he was hospitalized at the University of Michigan Hospital in Ann Arbor. None of the doctors, including the outstanding neurologists there, could offer any advice except that the cold wet Michigan winter and his multiple fall and spring allergies were aggravating his condition and that we should consider taking leave for the summer and spending it in a dry, warm area with clean air and away from the allergens of Michigan.

We decided on Phoenix, Arizona, because it was the only place in Arizona, Nevada, or New Mexico where we knew anyone. The Superintendent of Arizona State Hospital (the only institution in the entire state of less than 800,000 population which accommodated the mentally ill, alcoholics, senile, grossly retarded, and the "criminally insane" in a separate branch) was Dr. John Larson, an old friend, formerly a prominent Detroit psychiatrist and research physiologist. He had come out West for his young son's health and was running this small, minimally funded institution in antiquated buildings with a minimal, elderly medical staff; and was doing an incredibly able job of making it one of the most progressive and well-run institutions in the Southwest. Milton was pleased to be able to help. At the end of June, I drove out to Arizona with the four youngest children. The two older boys, then 17 and 19, stayed in Michigan. A few days after I left, Milton left the Ann Arbor hospital and was put on the plane by a friend to travel to Arizona, where Dr. Larson met him and put him up until I arrived a few days later. Milton was then recovering. We stayed at a motel a week, and then rented a small cottage for the summer.

During that time, I only recall one fairly short episode of relapse, and he felt so well he decided to join the State Hospital staff. I flew home for a few days and made moving arrangements, and on my return we moved to the hospital grounds. The 17-year-old son joined us by bus. Until spring of 1949, Milton worked hard, enthusiastically and with much energy, developing progressive changes at the State Hospital. Then Dr. Larson had a clash with a group of political members of the Arizona State Board of Control, resigned, and left the state. Milton resigned and decided to go into private practice.

We bought a house in Phoenix and were getting ready to move when he became severely but only briefly ill. He was hospitalized for a few days during the move, then came home and slowly regained strength while he gradually built up his practice. We originally intended to rent a regular office in a medical building but at this point I think he realized that he needed to exert himself physically less and rest more, so we realized the practical advantage of using a room in the house as a study and office where, when he had a free hour or so, he could go to bed if he wished. Therefore, from then until his death in 1980, his office was in the home.

In the fall of 1949, he was hospitalized twice—the recurrence was then considered to be a revival of the serum sickness, brought on by allergies to local allergens to which he had become sensitized, as well as dust and some foods. He had a very fine allergist who treated him for several years, recommending shots of antigens, as dust-free an environment as possible, and identification and avoidance of food sensitivities.

The next and the most severe episode was in 1953. The local doctors were sympathetic but had no recommendations. A medical friend at Johns Hopkins Hospital said he would have Milton admitted there for treatment if I could get him there. I could not go with him as I had two young children, born in 1949 and 1951, besides the other children still at home. Arrangements were made for two young medical interns to go with him by train; he was met by an ambulance, and the young men flew home.

Milton was hospitalized in Maryland for some time, recovering, and was examined by neurologists, orthopedists, and many other specialists. Then he seemed to be all right, but they still did not know of a diagnosis or a prognosis. They would have preferred to have him stay indefinitely for further testing, but he requested, and was given, a discharge and came home.

It was apparent that although he felt okay again, he had developed a lot of additional muscle impairment. Some months later, after he was well back into the schedule of work again, an orthopedist friend was visited by a renowned neurologist. This doctor examined Milton and said that in evaluating the recent muscle loss, he could make only one reasonable diagnosis, namely, a recent poliomyelitis attack, which would be rare but not impossible, since there are three strains of the virus.

In view of the recent findings of similar episodes in other polio victims (including recurrence of the original polio symptoms), this was a shrewd, medically astute, but possibly mistaken diagnosis.*

---

* Now being documented in persons who have had polio, this is being referred to as post-polio syndrome. Erickson's symptoms and episodes of illness were consistent with this syndrome.

During the remainder of Milton's life he did indeed have repeated episodes of illness, similar to the ones described. But after each episode, he was able to resume his work, traveled extensively, wrote papers, did research, and was active in organizational work and editing. Virtually every time, however, he actually lost some ground physically.

He lost the powerful shoulder muscles to such an extent that he frequently had to use both hands to raise an eating utensil. He used a wheelchair more and more—first only for extensive travel, then most of the time, using his cane to walk less and less frequently, eventually being completely restricted to a wheelchair. At that point, he gave up traveling (1969) and in 1970 we moved to another home, which was remodeled to make it practical for wheelchair living.

Between 1970 and 1980, he slowly lost muscular strength, developed some loss of tongue and cheek muscle control so he could no longer wear dentures nor speak as clearly, and lost ability to maintain prolonged eye-focus. He had to give up his extensive reading activity (of both professional and recreational literature). Still, his condition seemed to have stabilized, as I can only recall one fairly short episode (in 1970 or 1971) of severe illness.

He phased out his private practice of psychiatry, giving it up completely around 1974. By then, he was beginning to get requests for teaching sessions to be conducted at our home and office. These became so popular that he was actually booked up through the end of 1980, and could have been scheduled for the next year or so. He slowly cut down the teaching hours to afternoons only, five days a week, and future bookings were being made for four days a week.

This leads me to make another point: Although Dr. Erickson might be feeling very poorly, he would often pull himself together to give a very important lecture or to see a patient he felt was going through an acute psychiatric crisis and could not wait. He would then collapse into bed. But, in general, he would "pace" his strength, allow gaps in his schedule, go to bed for a rest; if he felt like reading, it might be very light (such as comic books).

In his last years, his recreation was watching television—he kept up on news of the day, loved natural history programs, and listened to commentators such as the "McNeil-Lehrer Report," but also relaxed with light programs from "Sesame Street" to "The Dukes of Hazzard."

He continued to contribute to professional literature by collaborating with Ernest Rossi and Jeffrey Zeig, but relaxed by scribbling off in pencil the long stories of animals and of family life that he told to his children and grandchildren. He told me that the light TV and the children's stories were beneficial to him as distractions from painful sensations.

He lived to be 78-years-old, far longer than he expected, and was active through the week before his death.*

Mrs. Erickson writes of her husband's very debilitating limitations; there were a score of other physical problems that could have lessened his enjoyment of life but because of his great buoyancy in overcoming them, they never did.

He was, for instance, born color-blind. However, instead of being restricted by it, he parlayed it into a rich vein of self-expression. He often wore purple clothing because this was the color he most appreciated. He had many purple decorations in his office and students often gave him purple gifts.

He was tone deaf; with progressive muscular loss, his vision became double; and his hearing was impaired. He was breathing by virtue of a few intercostal muscles and half a diaphragm; he had spinal arthritis, gout, and a touch of emphysema. When I first met him in 1973, he had limited use of his arms; in order to write, he sometimes had to guide his right hand with his more coordinated left hand. His use of his legs was severely limited; he could support himself only for the brief periods of time necessary to transfer himself from his wheelchair to his office chair. Around 1976, he stopped doing that and stayed in his wheelchair. Yet there was no bitterness or even resignation; Erickson satisfied himself with what he had.

When he was in his 70s, the mornings were especially hard for him. Sometimes it took so much energy to dress and shave that he would have to nap before he could see people. The pain seemed worse early in the day. His face showed it and he was open about discussing it. In 1974 he told me, "This morning I felt like I should have died at 4:00 a.m. By noon, I was glad to be alive and I've been glad ever since."

In spite of the tremendous physical problems, Erickson was one of the most glad-to-be-alive human beings one could ever expect to en-

---

* For additional biographical information see *Healing in Hypnosis* (Rossi, Ryan, and Sharp, 1983.)

counter. This aspect of his personality added greatly to his effectiveness as a therapist and teacher. There were also other facets of Erickson that were instrumental in his success.

## ABOUT ERICKSON: HIS PERSONAL STYLE IN RELATION TO HIS PROFESSIONAL LIFE

This is a book about Milton Erickson's unique contributions to psychotherapy, and the precise recounting of his poor health is meant to be more than anecdotal. Erickson's good cheer in the face of tremendous physical difficulties had a direct rehabilitative effect on his patients. They knew their problems could not be worse than his. They saw there was hope for a productive life no matter what obstacles they faced.

When patients who were suffering from schizophrenia, insecurity, or pain went to see Erickson, they walked into a room where they saw a therapist who was not speaking hypocritically or hypothetically. They saw a therapist who was struggling with pain and a tremendous number of limitations, but who was obviously enjoying life.

Erickson had a good sense of perspective about his situation. He used to say that poliomyelitis was the best teacher he ever had about human behavior (Zeig, 1980a, p. xx). He followed that up with, "I don't mind the pain—I don't like the alternatives." In addition to using self-hypnosis, he used his technique of "reframing" on himself. Perhaps some of his success with others came from the success he had using his techniques himself.

Also, Erickson's external orientation helped to control his own pain. He was alive to the environment (Zeig, 1980a, p. 16); he never seemed to get lost inside himself. When you were in his presence, you felt that all his attention was directed toward you. It was both flattering and comforting; at times it was unnerving.

Along with his orientation as an "interested observer," Erickson was characterized by a social aloofness. He was a private person, not ever the kind you would discuss current events or sports with.

But there was no aloofness when he was working; his contact was intense and personal. This is not to say that it made a person feel completely secure. Complete security is antithetical to change. Although I could bask in the security of his compassion, feeling that he was trying to help me develop my own talents in my own special way, I never felt fully on balance with him. People often felt "woozy" around Erickson (Zeig, 1980a, xxvii). Partly, this was because he was so conscious of having an impact on you (cf. Haley, 1982, p. 7). Yet it was "OK uncertainty." Even when you were off balance you felt that the uncertainty would lead to personal gain.

And it did. I remember that once I was scurrying around at a feverish 78 rpm, pressing to complete speaker scheduling for the 1980 International Congress on Ericksonian Approaches to Hypnosis and Psychotherapy. I asked him about including a particular speaker who was noted for integrating physical and psychological approaches. He said, "No, he has too much *tension* . . . in his body." His message was clearly two-pronged. I took a deep breath and slowed down to 33⅓ rpm. However, I didn't feel manipulated. I never felt manipulated with him; I felt better. (cf. Haley, 1982, p. 10, who also notes that there was no feeling of exploitation about Erickson.)

He was an incredibly confident person who didn't seem to know social fear (Nemetschek, 1982), and he was comfortable with power (Haley, 1982, p. 10). Yet there was a sense of play about him. He is credited as the first to introduce humor as a legitimate aspect of psychotherapy (Madanes, 1985). He also laced his inductions with humor. Traditionally, hypnosis and humor are considered immiscible. Erickson was the first to introduce humor as a legitimate aspect of hypnosis. For example, to a patient with arm levitation (Zeig, 1980a, p. 223), he playfully intoned, "Have you ever had a strange man lift your arm and leave it in midair before?"

When I think of how Erickson got things done with his patients, I am reminded of an incident concerning my infant daughter, Nicole, who hates to have her face washed after eating. My wife, Sherron, gave her the washcloth to entertain herself with. In the process, they accomplished the task without struggle, without intrusive force. Erickson's therapy seemed similar. It was adult play therapy (cf. Leveton, 1982). Like a good parent, he would encourage self-directed discovery. Credit for change was reserved for the patient.

Coupled with this sense of play was a sense of drama. Erickson had a bag full of unexpected tasks and tricks that he used to make a point (cf. Lustig, 1985). He would throw a styrofoam rock at a patient and exclaim, "Don't take anything for granite!" (C. Lankton, 1985). To demonstrate people's ignorance of familiar patterns, he would challenge them to prove whether they were right or left thumbed. (When you clasp your hands, the dominant thumb is on top. Then see how it feels to move all your fingers down one position.) To encourage flexibility, he would challenge students to conceptualize how to plant 10 trees in 5 rows of 4 trees each. (The solution to the problem is a five-pointed star.) He would send students and patients to climb Squaw Peak in Phoenix to get a vaster perspective, a higher point of view, and a feeling of triumph.

He would use himself as an example and cite difficult situations that he had turned into a game. As a high school student, he rewarded himself with geometry, which he enjoyed, for completing assignments he liked less. When he had to hoe a potato patch, he made diagonal lines across the field and then worked on different patches until the task was complete, thereby making it more interesting. And he got through life's necessary tedium while retaining the child's wonder at seeing the world. To one patient whom he wanted to be more playful, he quoted Wordsworth: "Shades of the prison house begin to close around the growing boy"—a lament about the loss of the innocence and appreciation of the child's perspective.

This childlike wonderment and trust had a natural extension that became the hallmark of his therapy: He had faith in people and in the healthful drives in their unconscious. He believed patients had innate wisdom that could be tapped. He told about helping a patient to take a professional exam by having the patient rapidly skim his textbooks and note one concept on each page, thereby priming his unconscious and eliciting memories. (I used this procedure successfully to take my state certifying exam.) He also had faith in the wisdom of his own unconscious. For example, he told a story about misplacing a manuscript and trusting the wisdom of losing it rather than searching for it. Sometime later he was rereading an article and found material that should have been included in the "lost" paper. Then he found it and published it (Zeig, 1985a).

Perhaps one reason Erickson was so interested in the subconscious—and in hypnosis—is that it bore so directly on his own pain-dogged life. He used hypnosis for pain control constantly. When Erickson did self-hypnosis for pain control, he didn't program himself; instead he set his unconscious on the idea of comfort and then followed up on the suggestions he received. He also told me about an elaborate signaling system he used. Upon arising in the morning in his later years, he would note the position of his thumb between his fingers. If it was between his pinky and ring finger, it meant he had controlled a lot of pain at night. If it was between his ring finger and middle finger, he had controlled less pain; if between his middle finger and fore finger, still less. In this way, he gauged how much available energy he would have for the day's work. He knew the unconscious can function benignly and autonomously.

Another gift Erickson brought to his practice was his massive creativity. Creativity kept him sharp. When I asked him a yes or no question, he often seemed to delight in finding a way to answer without saying the words "yes" or "no" even if the new answer was more lengthy. Margaret Mead (1977, p. 94) noted that he always strived to find original solutions and approached each session as if it were something entirely new. (Even though Erickson did repeat his stories and inductions, he was careful to modify them to fit the individual. He was not opposed to repetition. In an early supervisory session, he encouraged me to use one induction repetitively to learn the variation of responses.)

Perhaps his creativity and curiosity refreshed him. In his younger years, he seemed tireless. He would work long hours at home. When he traveled to lectures, he would often see colleagues, treat patients, and conduct individual therapy for workshop participants after hours. He had a remarkable memory and tremendous powers of concentration.

Erickson's humanism has not been fully developed in the literature, but it was a very important part of his therapy and an important part of his success. Perhaps one of the reasons he didn't seem manipulative in the pejorative sense was that he was so generous and thoughtful in his time and effort.

And in his generosity, he often displayed amazing attention to detail. An example comes to mind, reported in *A Teaching Seminar* (Zeig, 1980a, p. 312). When his 26th grandchild, Laurel, visited Phoenix as a newborn, Erickson had me take a picture. He also wanted in the picture the small ironwood owl that he had given the baby as her very first birthday gift. (Laurel's nickname was "Screech" because she had a powerful cry.) Erickson later commented to me that the owl added a tremendous amount of humanness to the picture, and that it would have a meaningful effect on teenaged Laurel when Erickson was long dead.

Every day in therapy, Erickson did unexpected things. You could almost count on him to do the opposite of what was expected. Haley (1982) discussed in detail how Erickson's practice was the opposite of what was done by traditional therapists. For example, it was not unusual for *him* to call up a patient and tell him to come for an appointment. In supervision, he encouraged students to do hypnosis in the first half of the session rather than waiting for the second half, as is common practice. It was not uncommon for him to conduct an induction upon initially meeting a student or patient and garner diagnostic information during the process of the induction.

As a man and a therapist, Erickson wasn't much interested in money. At the time of his death in 1980, his customary fee was only $40 per hour. If he had a group of students at a session, he would say, "If there are ten of you, each of you pay four dollars an hour; if you have more money, pay more. If you have less, pay less" (Zeig, 1980a). He admonished his students to request their fee at the end of each session, noting that this procedure encouraged the therapist to deliver, in return for which there would be immediate compensation. He came from the scientific school that if you had knowledge you shared it, you didn't sell it. On more than one occasion he said to patients, "I'm interested in your life, not your shekels."

This was the sort of almost folksy thing you expected him to say. His approach was pragmatic, down-to-earth. He used words that anyone could understand, but like the contemporary artist Paul Klee, the simple lines were deep and rich. His attention to detail in language was superb (cf. Rodger, 1982, p. 320) and it made his therapy rich. As will be seen from the transcript in the second half of this volume, he was remarkably articulate; for the most part he spoke in grammatically correct and complete sentences.

Yet Erickson was not intellectual in the way that you would think of an academician, although he was widely read. In particular, he had an exceptional memory and was especially well versed in literature, agriculture, and anthropology. In treating his patients he often used his knowledge of these fields.

## HOW ERICKSON TRAINED HIMSELF

Much of Erickson's life was a matter of creativity that he channeled into his family, his life, his work. But is such creativity just the undisciplined overspill of genius? Well, yes and no. Erickson possessed much personal genius, but his facility was also the product of diligent self-training. He went to school on his patients and had a wealth of experience to draw on from his years of clinical practice—by the time I met him, he had seen 50 of everything. He once asked a colleague, David Cheek, if Cheek knew where Erickson got his ongoing psychiatric knowledge. Cheek reported, "He said with his usual intonation, 'From patients' " (reported in Secter, 1982, p. 451). Being basically self-taught, Erickson was unencumbered by previous models and could blaze new trails. Erickson's medical school training in psychiatry at the University of Wisconsin in the early 1920s was under the direction of a surgeon who did not really believe in psychiatry. After medical school he did a one-year internship at the Colorado Psychopathic Hospital under Franklin Ebaugh, M.D., the Director of the hospital and a noted psychiatrist. However, Erickson never credited anyone as a teacher (Haley & Weakland, 1985, p. 603); he had no training or supervision in psychoanalysis, although he was well read in the area. He also taught himself hypnosis.

After medical school he used a number of methods to train himself. One major aspect of this self-education concerned the importance of socialization.

For years, Erickson would get a mental status examination on a patient and write out a hypothesized social history—that is, he would speculate what the patient's social history *could* be. Subsequently, he would get the real social history from the social work service and compare it with his intuited version. He also worked in the opposite direction by getting a real social history, composing a hypothesized mental status examination, and comparing it with a real mental status exam. He used this technique with numerous patients until he had a good understanding of social development.

Although Erickson worked primarily with individuals, he was an accomplished family systems thinker, and considered it an important aspect of therapy. For example, in 1974, I asked for advice in dealing with severely disturbed patients in a residential treatment center. The first thing he told me to do was to get data on the family constellation.

I expect that experts on family therapy can see a person and accurately describe the family systems and even psycho- and social-dynamics in past generations. As will be seen, Erickson had this ability and used it, as for example by creating powerful interventions by making predictions.

Erickson also worked hard to learn hypnosis. Early in his career, he would write out a 15-page induction for a particular patient, cut it down to ten pages, to five pages, to two pages, and then he would present it to the patient. He would even practice suggestions in a mirror (Hammond, 1984, p. 281). If one of his children's friends seemed like an interesting hypnotic subject, he would ask permission of the parents to work with that child, and he would conduct hypnotic experiments in the evening.

And even beyond his diligence, he was meticulous in his efforts. In 1939, Margaret Mead wrote a two-page letter to Erickson inquiring about hypnosis in relation to trance in primitive cultures. He replied with letters of 14 pages and 17 pages. His genius and diligence must have impressed her. The next year, Mead traveled to Michigan to meet Erickson, initiating a friendship that lasted until she died.

According to his sister, Bertha (personal communication, 1984), this pattern of hard work was always characteristic of him. He strived to master things at an early age. For example, as a child he was known as "Mr. Dictionary" because he read the dictionary many times and had a massive vocabulary.

But perhaps his brilliance was most startling in relationship to his awareness of nuance—and again, this was not an idle gift, but something he challenged himself to master. In his mature years, his power of observation was legendary. He would see a woman move in a particular way and think, "This woman is pregnant," even though there was no visible change in her figure. He would write down his prediction and give it to his secretary, who would seal it in a locked drawer. Then he would get confirmation of his observation.

His style of pushing himself to learn and improve continued into his later years. When his eyesight failed and he could no longer read, he watched television. One of his students reported that once there was a track meet on TV and that Erickson challenged himself to predict a winner. He watched the runners warming up. Some of them were looking around, distracted by the audience. He predicted that those people were not going to win. The ones who were really concentrating and focusing were going to be the winners.

A central facet of Erickson's personality was his interest in learning; he was one of the most voracious learners I have ever met. I once asked him if he ever got bored teaching the same stories week after week to the groups of students in attendance at his teaching seminars. He was incredulous. "Bored?" he said. "*No.* I am purely interested in what I can learn."

## THE CASE OF JOHN AND BARNEY

A chronicler can write forever and never reveal a man the way the man can reveal himself. Toward the end of his life, Milton Erickson took on a case that seemed a culmination of his own life and strengths, one that revealed him very clearly.

The case of John and Barney brought together Erickson's training, his greatest innovations and insights—the use of context, the ability to communicate for effect, his playfulness in therapy—with his great humanity.

Erickson began working with John in the early 1960s. John was suffering from schizophrenia, and it was clear this was going to be a long-term case. The goal was to keep John out of the hospital and enable him to have a productive life—not to cure him. When Erickson took on a patient, he would literally do anything he could to help the patient, whatever it took, as long as there was some real motivation for change. And so Erickson dug in and became involved with every aspect of John's life. One of Erickson's first interventions was to separate John, who was an only child, from his parents. This was done because it was judged, after initial sessions, that this family was not and could not be workable as a unit. The parents were instructed to establish a trust fund so that John would be financially independent and they were not to have contact with John. Each month Erickson got a small amount of money for John's treatment and John got a small stipend for living expenses.

At first John drove to sessions with Erickson, but after some time he couldn't drive because of his schizophrenia. So Erickson and Mrs. Erickson arranged for John to have an apartment within walking distance of the Erickson home.

As will be developed in the next chapter, goal-directedness is the cornerstone of the Ericksonian approach. What goals could Erickson have for this patient? Generally, there are four common patterns for schizophrenic patients:

1) They don't form satisfactory relationships.
2) They don't take responsibility.
3) They don't talk straight.
4) They don't like being defined into a particular role. For example, they are victims of life but they don't admit or acknowledge it.

Therefore, in conducting psychotherapy for schizophrenic patients, the goals are to get them to form relationships, take responsibility, talk straight, and assume productive roles. The problem in getting the patients to achieve these goals is that they rarely respond to direct suggestions. Generally they don't do many things directly—they triangulate in something else. For example, they communicate through their "voices," not directly.

If schizophrenics are experts at indirect or triangular communication, the therapist can communicate in a similar fashion, thereby meeting patients in their own frames of reference (cf., Zeig, 1980b). Erickson was going to accomplish indirect communication by getting John a dog. After John finally agreed to have a dog, Erickson sent Kristi, his youngest daughter and a medical student at the time, out with John to get one.

Now where do you get a dog for a schizophrenic patient? You don't go to a pet store and get a pedigreed dog. It just doesn't seem appropriate. An appropriate place to get a dog for a schizophrenic patient is the dog pound, an institution for chronic dogs who are awaiting their final shot of "Thorazine." Well, John walked into the pound, heard a bark, and immediately claimed a beagle puppy whom he named "Barney." John rescued Barney from institutionalization and imminent demise.

At first, Barney was kept in John's apartment, but soon it became clear that the apartment was too small for the dog. Where could he possibly keep him? Erickson volunteered to keep the dog at his home, but it wasn't going to be the Ericksons' dog—it was going to be John's dog. He was going to have to come over twice a day to feed and care for Barney.

Through the interactions with Barney, roles were subtly being redefined. John was no longer coming to Erickson's home as a patient—he was coming to care for the dog. In the process, he would take some steps toward responsibility.

Erickson even went a step further in the process of redefining roles. He stopped scheduling hourly appointments and John became a visiting friend of the family. Besides coming in the morning, John came every night from 8 o'clock to 10 o'clock and watched television with Dr. and Mrs. Erickson. John was exposed to family life while he was there, and Erickson could use his multiple-level communication to intersperse therapy. Some of Erickson's therapy involved "terrorizing" Barney and thereby cementing a relationship between John and Barney.

In the evenings, Erickson used a pair of pliers to break dog biscuits in half. (He had to use the pliers because he didn't have good use of his hands or the strength to break the dog biscuits without them. Even so, the task was difficult and his hands shook from the effort.) Mrs. Erickson could not be the one to break the dog biscuits and, if I was there, I couldn't be the one to break them. It had to be Erickson. He would give half the dog biscuit to John, who would then give it to Barney. If Barney came to Erickson, Erickson would wave a fly swatter at him, or would beep a horn which he had specially mounted on his wheelchair, and he would yell at Barney, "Shoo—John's dog!" (Erickson also used a soft approach. On occasions, he would look at

Barney and say, "Whose dog are you?" You could see John beam with pride.)

Let us consider the dynamics of the roles in this situation. If Erickson becomes the persecutor and Barney becomes the victim, it only leaves one position for John—the rescuer (cf. Karpman, 1968). And when John starts to be the rescuer he would also become more responsible. As a result of these interventions John has begun to break through his learned limitations.

Erickson's treatment of Barney was also lighthearted. He called Barney "that snake-bellied, Beagle-mix hound dog." According to Erickson, Barney's name for Erickson was "the Old Codger," and Barney called Mrs. Erickson "the Lady of the House."

Having gotten all these identities down, Erickson started to write letters from Barney to John. Erickson was for communicating by any possible means, and one can certainly write letters therapeutically. And it is another example of using therapeutic triangular communication with a schizophrenic. (Letters were also part of the Erickson tradition. It seems that Erickson's dog Roger wrote to Robert Pearson's dog, Pepper, informing Dr. Pearson about the cases his master was seeing [Pearson, 1982, p. 426]. Roger was certainly prolific; Dr. John Corley's dog also got letters [Corley, 1982, p. 237] and so did Dr. Bertha Roger's dog [personal communication, 1984]. After Roger died, Ghost Roger wrote letters to the family from the "out beyond" and his correspondence was circulated to the Erickson children and grandchildren. These letters were Erickson's ways of parenting; they discussed incidents involving the extended family and incorporated ideas about moral development and enjoying life.)

So Barney started writing letters and John not only became a visiting friend but now he was an "adopted" member of the Erickson family.

Here is a letter from 1972. It was handwritten, a painstaking task for Erickson:

May, 1972

Dear John:
   I got up early this morning. It was such a nice day, but something puzzles me. Saturday, Robert (Erickson's youngest son) was telling Kathy (Erickson's daughter-in-law) a story, and the Lady of the House was listening, too. It was a story about some

old codger who advertised for a wife and he got a letter of application. He went down to the airport with two horses to get her. On the way to the preacher's place, his horse stumbled and the old codger just said, "One." Halfway there, the horse stumbled again, and the old codger said, "Two." Just when they got to the preacher's place, his horse stumbled again. The old codger got down from his horse, unsaddled him, said, "Three." Then he shot the horse dead right there. The bride-to-be said, "Why that's outrageous to shoot a horse just for stumbling." The old codger just said, "One."

I didn't hear the rest of the story, but I did hear the Lady of the House whisper, "Be sure you don't tell that story to you know who." What does that mean, John?

Barney

The next day there was another letter. As you read it, note Erickson's multilevel interspersal technique, by which he simultaneously communicated more than one thing. He reframed the idea of being crazy by using synonyms of the word "crazy" attached to positive emotions. Also, in a humorous and dramatic fashion he made light of fear, an emotion that John was certainly familiar with. In a compassionate way, he even suggested that John could not expect to totally surmount his problems. He emphasized John's bond with Barney and introduced an alliance with Mrs. Erickson, who would also have a role as Barney's protector. And throughout the whole process, he obviously enjoyed himself.

May 1972

Dear John:

You know how I feel about that wonder girl Roxie [Erickson's second-to-youngest daughter]. She didn't come home this weekend—didn't even send a small bone to comfort me. I got to feeling so bad I tried to comfort myself. I quietly slipped into Kristi's room. I was really getting to feel good, dreaming wonderful dreams about Roxie patting me on the head and giving me a nice juicy bone and, wouldn't you know it, the Old Codger came along and saw me. I was enjoying my dream so much I didn't hear his wheelchair. It was awful, just awful, John. He came in with that terrible horn of his, and in a most ominous, threatening tone of voice, he said, "One." Then that horn turned my bones into quivering jelly. I trembled and shook so bad, so awful bad, I couldn't run out of the room. I just trembled and finally I slithered out and the Lady of the House kindly opened the back door and I sort of fell outside. It took me over an hour to get my tail out from between my legs where it got sort of stuck to the jelly that awful horn turned my lovely snake belly into. And it took hours to get it into wagging condition. John, it was the awfulest experience of my whole life—that is, I just thought it was. Now, John, you know how plumb loco I am on that girl, Roxie, and Kristi sometimes just drives me out of my mind with her nice ways. And the Lady of the House can make me careless and abounding with the joy of life. And you have made me so aware of the majesty of dogness with the Bay Rum baths you give me in your apartment and just being Your Dog, your very own dog. Well, John, all these wonderful things you have brought into my life made me off-balance after what the Old Codger did to me. I got to thinking about how anybody so nice as the Lady of the House ever let herself get tied to such a thing as the Old Codger and well, it must be that I wasn't thinking too straight and somehow I wandered into the bedroom where the Old Codger sleeps but I was beside the bed where the Lady of the House sleeps—I just desperately needed some comfort. And the Old Codger caught me again. In an awful, awful way, he said, "Two," before he started with the horn. I thought that the first time was terrible but I now know what sheer stark devastating terror is. Luckily for me the Lady of the House rushed in and saved me. I couldn't move, I was completely done in. The Lady of the House saved my life. I thought I would never see my wonderful John again or Roxie, or have another Bay Rum bath and walks with My John. Just plain nothingness was staring me in the face.

Now, John, I know that a codger like the Old Codger doesn't offer much chance for improvement, but I'm willing for you to give him all the chew sticks and pork chops you bring me. I'm willing to give up my signing rights—just anything—so that I can keep on being John's dog and be plumb loco about Roxie.

Barney

Then Erickson took to writing poems. I found a series of 44 limericks that Erickson gave as a holiday gift, entitled "Limericks for Barney" by the Old Codger, 1973. They were about John's role as Barney's protector; ego building for John; about enjoying life and having proper values; and about Erickson's family, thereby engendering more of a sense of belonging in John. Here are a few of the limericks:

That wonderful secretary named Pinky
And that brown-tick beagle-mix so slinky
Both by Ghost Roger
And the Old Codger
Are being driven completely to drinkee

John is a handsome fellow,
And when it's time to say "Hello"
Barney waits
At the Gates
And then pretends to be cool and mellow.

There is something I would sorta
Like to say to my dear daughta
Although she is sweet
And also very neat
She does to my pensions what she hadn't oughta.
(Now how did this limerick get here?)

Now Barney is a fortunate dog
Who many miles up Squaw Peak did jog
But he does have one fault
Which no one can halt
It's this—all of John's affection he does hog.

The Old Codger's table creaks
There follow those wheelchair squeaks
From his haven
Very craven
Alert Barney, all tippytoes, retreats.


John the Wonderful has a hound
That he happily rescued from the pound
For him John does choose
Various things called chews
Barney thinks that it's wonderful to have John around.

A few weeks after Erickson died, Barney died. Barney was a medical wonder; he had disseminated Valley Fever. Mrs. Erickson made many trips to the veterinarian's office and spent hundreds of dollars to keep the dog alive, functioning well and happily between recurrences of the disease, because he was so important to John. In fact, Barney was such an unusual case, the veterinarian discussed it at a symposium on coccidioidomycosis in animals.

After Barney's death, Mrs. Erickson went with John and they found two beagle-mix puppies from the same litter. John named his new dog Barnabus; Mrs. Erickson named her new dog Angelique. She calls her "little angel." Now they both have new dogs—new symbols, new objects to love.

Every night from 8 o'clock to 10 o'clock, John still comes to the Erickson home and watches television with Mrs. Erickson. The role Erickson meticulously nurtured has been extended; now John is Mrs. Erickson's friend and views himself as her rescuer and protector. They take walks daily, and when she travels he watches the house and cares for the dogs.

Erickson had the goal of changing John's role and building satisfactory relationships. He took small, manageable steps toward this task, and continued to build relentlessly until success was achieved. Erickson provided John with some reference experiences for being responsible and taking on a new role. Subsequently, he "braided" those experiences together. Throughout the process, indirect communication was utilized. His goals were not great. He didn't think that John would have a normal social or vocational adjustment. However, he would have a more productive and fulfilling life within the protection of the Erickson family.

This case is a good example of how Erickson planned ahead and set up responses that could be used in the future. I once talked to Carl Whitaker, the noted family therapist, about Erickson. He said, "That Erickson must have had some left hemisphere." At the time I said, no, that he was probably a very intuitive chap. After studying more about Erickson, I agree—he must have had some left hemisphere.

## ERICKSON'S STYLE

The most amazing aspect of this story is that Erickson's efforts in this case were not unusual. For example, if he was going to do an induction of hypnosis, he might send his children out to the patient's home to learn what it was like to walk up the patient's front steps. In doing the induction, Erickson would create a fantasy about walking up steps. Pretty soon the patient would realize that Erickson was talking about his home.

I remember one former patient of Erickson's who was being battered by her husband. Erickson told her that her husband was possibly homicidal and that she should leave her hometown and move to Phoenix. He even said he would lend her money to get started. The woman didn't follow his advice but she knew Erickson meant what he said. The extent to which he would help motivate patients seemed almost limitless.

One woman was a patient of his for more than 13 years. She suffered from acute episodic hysterical psychoses, and she would see Erickson whenever she had a psychotic episode. Then she would go out and live her life independent of therapy. The therapy was directed to keeping her out of the hospital, living as productively as possible.

This patient also went through an alcoholic stage during which Erickson sent his son Robert to check out her home to make sure she wasn't hiding any alcohol—Robert is good at finding things. Then he sent his then teenage daughters, Kristina and Roxanna, to babysit with the patient to make sure she didn't drink. Erickson wanted to avoid psychiatric hospitalization if at all possible.

The patient was dominated by her mother. During a consultation, Erickson confronted the mother about getting out of her daughter's life. She was so infuriated that she walked ten miles from Erickson's home to the airport. There was an iron fist under Erickson's velvet glove, and he certainly could be direct—yet he maintained a relationship with the mother. His confrontation was taken as a sign of his strength, not as an insult. (The patient was not Caucasian and Erickson was making his confrontation on the basis of his understanding of the mores of her ethnic group.)

To the same extent that Erickson's therapy was characterized by innovation, it was also characterized by informality. When he lived on Cypress Street, from 1949 to 1970, his office was in his home and the waiting room was in his living room. The house had four bedrooms: one for the boys, one for the girls, one for Dr. and Mrs. Erickson, and one that served as Erickson's office (which Jay Haley said was the size of a postage stamp). The patients waited in the living room and played with the children. The secretary typed on the dining room table and Erickson's office was behind the dining room.

This was the Ericksonian approach to family therapy. Erickson's family did therapy with the patient. The family never thought of doing otherwise; it was just a part of being an Erickson.

I hope these stories and recollections have somehow illustrated Erickson's humanistic approach to therapy. I know that sometimes his cases read like O. Henry short stories that build to a denouement, then twist suddenly to reveal Erickson's method. And I know that Erickson often seems like a technician who effects rapid cures. But the magic, like all magic, is primarily an illusion. Erickson put an extreme amount of energy into his patients, showing them repeatedly that he was willing to extend himself to help. And knowing someone cares is a primary force behind recovery.

# CHAPTER 2

# The Ericksonian
# Approach

---

Ericksonian methods are probably the fastest-growing field of psychotherapy in the western world. In December, 1980, and in December, 1983, the International Congresses on Ericksonian Approaches to Hypnosis and Psychotherapy each brought together some 2,000 professionals from more than 20 nations; the Congresses were the largest meetings ever held on the topic of hypnotherapy. They demonstrated that hypnotherapy has finally entered the mainstream and that Erickson's work represented an enduring departure from established psychotherapeutic tradition.

## ERICKSON'S DEPARTURE FROM CONTEMPORARY
## TRADITIONS

Psychology has always been a science dedicated to the question of "Why?" The question "How?" has been nearly altogether missing. And when we look closely, we see that this orientation is the result of a European tradition that often exalts theory and experimental research above clinical results. More than any single individual, Milton Erickson has reoriented psychotherapy toward results.

Let us take a brief glance backwards at medical history. Chauvinism in the United States is such that we think of psychology as an American invention, independent of its European roots. This attitude is reinforced by the fact that since World War II most European psychologists have turned their heads to the West for the definitive word on matters of the mind. And because European graduate education is more theoretical than practical, at any given time many American trainers are teaching clinical work in Europe.

On closer examination, however, we realize that American psychology and psychotherapy are young sciences steeped in the European tradition. Psychology is composed of three parts—theoretical, experimental, and clinical efforts—but the search for theoretical formulations and experimental evidence has predominated. Most psychotherapists have based their clinical practice on the search for causes, whether biochemical, intrapsychic or interpersonal. They have asked, "Why?"

Although American pragmatism based on "How" has led to original contributions in scientific and technical fields, the attitude of "How" has been absent in the psychotherapy clinic (cf. Haley, 1982). Therapists and patients discuss the past, "why" the problem exists. Most psychotherapy has been archeology, a search for the "buried treasure" of the psyche that explains how "aberrations" develop, often assuming that such explanations in themselves could cause change. But it is inadequate to think that analyzing how a structure was built can cause any change in its function.

Still, many psychotherapists have been content merely to understand, describe and theorize; promoting change is often relegated to second place. It is considered "higher-level" to create theory and conduct experiments. As far as having an effect on the patient is concerned, practitioners generally have been satisfied with developing rote procedures that can be universally applied without consideration of the fact that each person thinks, feels and acts in a unique manner. (Erickson compared such approaches to an obstetrician delivering every baby with forceps [Zeig, 1982, p. 255].)

In contradistinction, the arts—literature, poetry, painting, theatre and music—have developed as forms of influence. The most effective artists are those who are best able to use the tools of their trade to powerfully influence mood and perspective. Therapists could benefit from this example.

But perhaps it is not an example closely enough keyed to their own work to inspire them. In fact, the prevailing emphasis on theory may be due to the fact that before Milton Erickson there was never a model showing that it was possible therapeutically to *use* all of the output channels of communication—words, voice, tone, body posture, etc.—and tailor them to an individual to effect change.

Erickson was not only the first model, he was a very remarkable one. His communication was precise and his therapies could be analyzed word for word, movement for movement. He wasted little effort and each element of his communication was a tool designed to have therapeutic effect.

Where most psychotherapists have learned to be listeners, Erickson trained himself to be a communicator. If he changed the direction of his voice or moved his hand, he was aware of the potential effect and ready to build on the response of his patient.

Erickson was a man interested in change, not theory. He thought of explicit personality theory as a hindrance that limits practitioners to thinking about circumscribed problems and rules rather than freeing them to perceive and utilize personal and interpersonal differences. He said that he didn't understand why people made up comprehensive theories of personality. Each personality is different. When using a theory, one listens for proof of the theory; we listen for what we want to hear. He gave me an example by listing some words—saddle, stable, hay, house, bridle—and pointed out the tendency to read "house" as "horse." He knew that we have a tendency to functional fixedness and should strive to overcome factors that induce and maintain limitations.

To help his patients do so, he became the master of individualized multilevel communication. We know that psychotherapy occurs whenever a significant change is made in the habitual pattern of maladaptive behavior (Zeig, 1982, p. 258). Change can be effected by working with the symptom, the personality, the social system, or any combination of these factors. There are systemic reverberations from strategic change. For example, if the symptom is modified, there is generative change in the personality and social system (cf. C. Lankton, 1985). Alternately, as the therapist changes personality and social reactions, the symptom changes. Whatever the fulcrum—be it the symptom, the personality, the system—the lever that induces change is individualized multilevel communication.

And Erickson used it like no other.

## MULTILEVEL COMMUNICATION

The main tool of the Ericksonian method is psychological level (indirect) communication (cf. Lankton, Lankton & Brown, 1981; Lankton & Lankton, 1983). Haley (1982, p. 7) noted that one of Erickson's greatest skills was his ability to influence people indirectly. He was like a watchmaker who would reach around and tinker with the back of the clock to subtly make it function again. He normally wouldn't shake it to make it work (Zeig in Van Dyck, 1982, p. 40).

In pioneering indirect techniques, Erickson noted that communication occurs on multiple levels, including the verbal content, the nonverbal behavior, and the implications of each. Indirect communications are, in fact, implications, not overt content; indirection is a process whereby responses are effected without full awareness on the part of the subject (Zeig, 1985a). So facile was Erickson with multiple level communication that he could have a personal and private conversation with a demonstration subject without the knowledge of the audience (Haley, 1982).

Some experts maintain that only a small fraction of responses to communication are due to the verbal content. Most responses are due to subconscious perceptions of implication. In studying communication, one perceives that the effect of the message is of paramount importance, not the cleverness of the technique or the possible meanings inherent in the message. Outcome prevails over structure.

All of this Erickson understood. He combined this knowledge with a utilization of the patient's own values to both guide internal associations and make changes in context until there was a sufficient supply of associations to allow patients to voluntarily effect change to their own credit (Zeig, 1980a, p. 11). From the beginning of therapy, he considered patients to be complete, as having the necessary resources to accomplish the therapy. The task of Erickson's therapy—and of those therapists who have been influenced by him—is to help patients access previously unrecognized potentials for change.

And in doing so, Erickson behaved like no therapist who came before. He broke with tradition on all sides.

Traditionally, therapy is based on analysis and understanding. According to one's theoretical orientation, the therapist interprets back to the patient what the patient "really means." Usually this involves confronting and analyzing weaknesses and deficits. Having had beneficial training in each of the following therapy approaches, I can provide some overly simplified, somewhat humorous examples. For example, if the patient enters the consulting room and says, "It's really a beautiful day," the psychoanalyst might say, "You're treating me in an awfully familiar fashion. I wonder if you're confusing me with someone from your past." Then the practitioner would work through the transference aspects of the relationship. (It is the bane of analysts that, unfortunately, life distorts the transference.)

If the therapist were a Transactional Analyst, in response to the same communication he might say, "Well, I recognize this sequence; it is the beginning of a past time which will lead to a game and your bad feeling racket. That will advance your tragic life-script of being a loser—so, talk straight."

A Gestaltist might handle the situation differently and reply, "Aha, here is a split. Put the day on the empty chair, talk to the 'day,' then be the 'day' and talk to yourself."

In each case the essence of psychotherapy is interpretation. The patient is speaking on multiple levels, unaware of what is really being communicated. And ostensibly the job of the therapist is to promote understanding, either of the structure of the past or of the structure of the present.

But one can appreciate the flowers rather than speculating about the seeds (Zeig, 1985a, p. 318). The Ericksonian approach maintains that if patients are intelligent enough to say things on one level and mean many others, psychotherapists should be equally intelligent and be able to say one thing and simultaneously mean other things that have directed therapeutic value (Zeig, 1980a, xxviii).

Using therapeutic multilevel communication is not a new idea. Eric Berne (1966, p. 227) argued that every communication consists of a social level and a psychological level. Similarly, Bateson & Ruesch (1951, pp. 179-181) said each communication contains a report and a command. Watzlawick (1985) posited that each communication is indicative and injunctive. It is generally known that communications don't merely provide information; they also tell the listener to "do something." But Erickson capitalized on this knowledge; his approach utilized the injunctive aspect of communication because it is this aspect that is therapeutic. Therefore, therapy is no longer based on understanding; it is based on effect.

For the therapist using psychological level influence communication, the therapeutic communication can be obtuse, indirect, metaphoric, and illogical, and consist of seemingly irrelevant tasks. It does not need to be concrete, logical and to the point, all of which Erickson understood to be unnecessarily limiting.

In one sense, Erickson's method was a therapy of courtesy and politeness (Haley & Weakland, 1985).* If the patient is talking on multiple levels, it is not only potentially ineffective but impolite to barge in and inform him or her that he is speaking on multiple levels that need to be analyzed and understood.

For example, if a patient comes in with somatic problems and the therapist suspects an underlying depression, he could confront the patient with, "Well, you really don't have physical problems. What you're really suffering from is depression, and I want to treat you for that." But an Ericksonian therapist might be polite by talking about somatic problems, and also might intersperse, on multiple levels, communications and tasks that set up a context for the person to access resources and realize potentials for change. This approach is more effective partly because it respects the patient's denial. We all

---

* As will be seen in the transcript in the case of the alcoholic (12/5/73), Erickson could use rudeness as a therapeutic ploy.

engage in self-deception, and there are psychological benefits to the veil of denial that is the shroud of self-deception. Piercing it is often unnecessary, but if it is necessary, finesse is preferable to a battering ram; it engenders less disruption and less resistance.

## THE PLACE OF TECHNIQUE

Erickson was opposed not only to theory but also to rigid "cookbook" techniques. Rather than discussing specific techniques, he preferred to promote the idea of "utilization."

"Utilization" basically says that techniques are best derived from the patient, not from the therapist. Whatever technique the patient uses to be an ineffective patient can be used by the therapist to promote effective living. For example, if the patient "speaks schizophrenic" to distance himself, the therapist can use the same method to promote an empathic relationship. Utilization says that it is best not to bend the patient to fit a preselected technique; rather, one should tailor psychotherapy to each patient (Zeig, 1982, p. 255).

Beyond utilization, Erickson's therapies were characterized not by techniques, but by some general attitudes about therapy—and for that matter, about life. One of these was flexibility in approach. Erickson would use whatever it took to promote change, be it interpretation, indirect suggestion or hypnosis. (Kristina Erickson, M.D., Erickson's youngest daughter, defined the Ericksonian approach as "that which works.") In his later years, he even kept flexible hours. The length of the session was determined by the goal, not by the clock. He would see patients for ten minutes or four hours and then usually charge accordingly.

Another attitude that set his therapy apart was the ability to think ahead. He would have in mind an intended effect and a method to achieve it.

And he was personally oriented to the future. Four months before he died, I unexpectedly asked him, "What's your goal?" Unhesitatingly he replied, "To see Roxanna's (his daughter's) baby." His 26th grandchild, Laurel, was born a few weeks later.

When one goal was achieved, he would set new goals. In similar fashion to his father who planted some young fruit trees while in his

90s, the week before he died Erickson made sure that Mrs. Erickson had bought several kinds of vegetable seeds and expressed concern that the spring garden hadn't been planted early enough.

Erickson often intoned, "Life is lived in the present and directed toward a future." Unfortunately, strategic goal directiveness is not part of the training of most therapists.

Although goal directed, he did not normally think about applying specific interventions. His mentality was flexible: Where is the patient now? Where can the patient get to? What resource does the patient have to accomplish the transition? What could Erickson best do to facilitate eliciting the resource, and the realization of the therapeutic goal? His orientation was to strengthen what is right with the patient rather than analyzing deficits.

## The Utilization Approach

Where others paid lip service to the idea of utilizing resources, Erickson actually followed through on this concept.

The process of psychotherapy is most important. Any intervention must be properly timed and seeded, and a proper follow-through must be accomplished. (One of my students, Robert Schwartz, Psy.D., named this methodology SIFT—Seed, Intervene, Follow Through.) Erickson understood the process to be delicate, and utilized aspects of the patient's personality to effect interventions in small steps. He did not merely present the main intervention. Rather, he usually divided a task into a number of steps and got the patient to agree to one step. The small steps could then be "braided" together. And by the time the main intervention was presented, it was just one small step in a chain of steps to which the patient had already agreed.

It is antithetical to the Ericksonian approach to provide a model of his treatment. However, I can identify important issues in the utilization approach:

1) Identify the resource (unaccessed strengths) in the patient.
2) Diagnose the patient's values, i.e., what the patient likes and dislikes (which also can be resources).
3) Develop the resource by utilizing the patient's values. (For

additional information on identifying and utilizing values, see Yapko, 1985.) The high "hit rate" Erickson enjoyed for his suggestions was due to his perceptiveness, attention to detail, and especially to his use of patients' values.

4) Connect the developed resource to the problem, either directly or indirectly.

5) Step four is best conducted by moving in small steps, accessing trust, rapport and motivation and guiding responsiveness throughout the process. Erickson believed that patients learn best when they do things. Therapeutic actions must be relevant to the patient and his or her values.

6) Any behavior, even resistance, can be accepted and utilized therapeutically. Any aspect of the context can be accepted and utilized therapeutically.

7) Drama can be used to enhance responsiveness to directives.

8) Seeding ideas prior to presenting them primes responsive behavior.

9) Timing is crucial. The process of therapy involves pacing, disrupting and patterning. Resistance often results from inadequate attention to these processes.

10) The therapist (and patient) must have an expectant attitude. Here are some examples:

a) There is a story that may be apocryphal about an experimenter who asked a graduate student to conduct some research. The graduate student was to go into a room where he would find two undergraduates and give one of them a dime and the other a dollar. No information was provided about which student was to receive the dime and which student was to receive the dollar.

Unbeknownst to the graduate student, the experimenter met privately with each of the undergraduate students prior to the experiment. One was told that the graduate student would give him a dime; the other was told that the graduate student would give him a dollar.

Of course, the student who expected the dollar usually got the dollar (Zeig, 1982, p. 262).

Expectation and conviction do not ensure results.

However, it does help to have a full dollar's expectations for one's patients.

b) Schoen (1983) reported a case of a patient who had previous therapy but was unable to overcome a habit problem. After one year of visits to Erickson, the patient succeeded. When asked how he got over the problem, he indicated, "Erickson *believed* that I could conquer it."

c) Mrs. Erickson (personal communication, September 1984) remembered an occasion when Erickson conducted psychotherapy in a social situation. They were in an airplane where the seats faced each other. The man across from them caught on to the fact that Erickson was a well-known psychiatrist. Mrs. Erickson reported:

> *He mentioned quite diffidently and respectfully that he was not looking forward to the trip because he was always terribly nauseated on an airplane ride. He wondered if Dr. Erickson would have any suggestions. And Milton, very solemnly, told him how he could hold his thumb in a particular way. As soon as he felt nausea, pain, or nervousness, he would press his thumb until it really started to be painful. When he did that, he would find that the feelings would back off.*
>
> *I remember sitting there staring as he explained this method thinking, "How could this work? Milton knows absolutely nothing about this guy. How could it possibly work?"*
>
> *And, by golly, two or three times during the flight, I saw that man grimace very discreetly. When they served lunch, he ate a hearty meal.*

11) Follow through. This basically involves testing the effectiveness of the intervention. One technique is to have the patient practice the new behavior in the room with the therapist. Another is to have follow-up contact with the patient. A third is to have the patient practice the new behavior in fantasy. Follow-through and seeding are microscopic as well as macroscopic; each step of the therapy sequence can be seeded and tested to ensure that a therapeutic response is elicited.

As can be seen, often therapy entails getting patients to do what they want to do if it is achievable. Sometimes it involves surmounting developmental obstacles. It is neither the cure of all past, present and future difficulties nor is it awareness or growth. "Growth" is not dependent on therapy; it is independent of it.

Erickson's approach was not to believe that his patients could be cured for all time, but rather to assume that in the short run they would surmount an immediate problem. They could come back for more therapy at a later time if need be. In the process, valuable problem-solving skills could be mastered.

However, his therapy was not just short-term; he did have contact with patients over time when long-term therapy was indicated. This extended treatment was still goal-directed.

The case of Joe, one of Erickson's most famous, provides an example of his action-oriented approach. (This case and the ethics of it are described in more detail in Zeig, 1985b. It is also cited and reported in more detail in Haley, 1973.) Note how the 11 processes in the utilization approach are used in an interconnected and nonlinear fashion.

### The Case of Joe

Erickson (1966) reported the use of an informal method of hypnotic, psychological-level communication—the interspersal technique. In this instance, it was used for pain control.

Joe was a florist who suffered from terminal cancer. Heavy doses of pain medication caused toxicity but supplied little relief. Erickson was asked by a relative to see Joe in the hospital, and to use hypnosis for pain control. Shortly before meeting Joe, Erickson was informed that Joe disliked even the word "hypnosis." Moreover, one of Joe's children, a resident in psychiatry who did not believe in hypnosis, was also present at the time of Erickson's introduction to Joe. Joe knew of his son's disbelief.

When Erickson met Joe in the hospital, he doubted that Joe really knew why Erickson was there. Joe could not talk to Erickson because of a tracheotomy and communicated by writing. Erickson began his therapy, which lasted a full day, by stating

Joe, I would like to talk with you. I know that you are a florist, that you grow flowers, and I grew up on a farm in Wisconsin and I liked growing flowers. I still do. So, I would like to have you take a seat in that easy chair as I talk to you. I'm going to say a lot of things to you but it won't be about flowers because you know more than I do about flowers. *That isn't what you want.* [*Italics are used here to denote interspersal and hypnotic suggestions which may be syllables, words, sentences, or phrases uttered with a slightly different intonation.*]

Now as I talk, and I can do so *comfortably,* I wish that you will listen to me *comfortably* as I talk about tomato plants. That is an odd thing to talk about. It makes one *curious. Why talk about a tomato plant?* One puts a tomato seed in the ground and he *will hope* that it will grow into a tomato plant that *will bring satisfaction* by the fruit it has. The seed soaks up water, *with not very much difficulty.* In doing that, because of the rains that *bring peace and comfort.* . . . (Erickson, 1966, p. 203)

Joe responded to the interspersed suggestions in the monologue about tomato plants and subsequently left the hospital, gained weight and strength, and used less medication for pain. Erickson saw Joe a second time and again used his indirect technique.

## Commentary

Erickson (personal communication, March 4, 1976) commented on the case:

Joe's wife, daughter, brother-in-law all listened [as I conducted therapy], and finally his wife intruded to ask me to start hypnosis. She was startled to discover that it had been done. What I had been saying to Joe they all thought to be nonsense. . . .

When you examine an abdomen for possible appendicitis, you begin the examination at that point of the abdomen most removed from the appendical area, slowly approaching the critical area.

. . . I started as far away from Joe's cancer as I could, without trying to identify it. Indeed, I said a lot of words that Joe translated into the experiential learnings that he thought he had lost forever until he built up a sufficient supply of his good associations to replace the things he didn't want. [*The entire letter from which this is excerpted is reported in Zeig, 1985b, pp. 464-466*]

Erickson realized that Joe had unrecognized learnings that made pain control possible. He used Joe's values by discussing plants. He incorporated drama and provided a frame that would fix Joe's attention and thereby begin to associate Joe away from discomfort. The essential communication was indirect, building in small steps. Concepts were presented and subsequently developed. The habitual maladaptive pattern (pain) was disrupted and a new pattern (comfort) was elicited. Erickson did not confront or analyze either the patient's need for pain or his resistance to treatment. In fact, he neither introduced himself as an agent of change nor formally hypnotized the patient. But he did show the patient "how to" be different.

## The Case of Barbie

A parallel example concerns a case of anorexia reported in Zeig, 1985c. The actual transcript of the session is presented in *A Teaching Seminar with Milton H. Erickson* (Zeig, 1980a).

Erickson did not immediately agree to see Barbie. In the initial phone call from her mother, he said that he would have to think over the situation; she was to call again in a few days. When she did, Erickson agreed to take the case and told the mother to bring her daughter to Phoenix.

During the first two interviews, the mother answered most of the questions that Erickson put to Barbie. On the third day, she complained that Barbie kept her awake at night by whimpering softly. Erickson confronted Barbie who agreed that she should be punished for the offense. Erickson privately told the mother to punish Barbie by making her eat two scrambled eggs. At the same session, in Barbie's presence, he confronted the mother and told her to let Barbie answer questions for herself.

In subsequent sessions, Erickson told Barbie stories. The anecdotes concerned many life situations; some were about Erickson's childhood. However, each story contained references to food. After two weeks in Arizona, the mother suggested that she and Barbie visit the Grand Canyon. Erickson told Barbie that he was supposed to look after her health and made her promise to brush her teeth and use mouthwash twice a day. He told her she could use any fluoride toothpaste but she was to use raw cod liver oil as a mouthwash.

In a subsequent session, Erickson confronted the mother about her own weight. He said that she was below normal weight and gave Barbie the task of telling him immediately if mother did not clean her plate. One day Barbie said that she forgot to tell Erickson that mother didn't finish her meal. Erickson punished them both by making them come to his house to eat cheese sandwiches.

Barbie and mother agreed with Erickson as to the goal weight they could have before leaving Phoenix. Erickson suggested weights and Barbie chose from the alternatives he offered. When they reached their goal, father came to Phoenix with the rest of the family. Erickson chided him for being five pounds underweight because it might have a detrimental effect on Barbie. Here is how he handled the other family members and Barbie.

> I called in the two older siblings and said, "When did Barbie first begin to get sick?" They said about a year ago. "How did she show it?" They said, "When any of us tried to give her any food, a fruit or candy or a present, she always said, 'I don't deserve it, keep it for yourselves.' And so we did." So, I read them the riot act for depriving their sister of her constitutional rights. I pointed out to them that Barbie had the right to *receive* the present regardless of what use she made of it. Even if she threw it away, she had the right to receive. "You selfish people kept the gift for yourselves just because she said she didn't deserve it. You robbed your sister of her right to receive gifts." And they were duly rebuked. I sent them out and had Barbie come in.
>
> I said, "When did you first begin to get sick, Barbie?" She said, "Last March." I asked, "How did you show your sickness?" She said, "Well, when anybody offered me food, fruit or candy or presents, I always said, 'I don't deserve it. Keep it for yourself.' " I said, "I am ashamed of you, Barbie. You robbed your siblings and your parents of their right to give you something. It didn't make any difference what you did with them, with the gifts, but they did have the right to give the gift to you, and you robbed them of their right to give you gifts and I am ashamed of you. You ought to be ashamed of yourself."
>
> And Barbie agreed that she should have allowed her parents and siblings to give her gifts. Not that she had to use them, but that they had the right to give them to her no matter what she did with them (Zeig, 1980a, pp. 140-141).

Barbie went home and sent Erickson pictures of her progress. In each letter there was an indirect reference to food. She gained weight and made an adequate adjustment.

## Commentary

I can comment on this case personally because I discussed it with Erickson, and I met Barbie. It is possible that Erickson did not agree to see them immediately in order to increase expectancy and motivation. When I asked Erickson why he allowed Barbie's mother to answer for her for two days before confronting her, he replied that he waited until he had rapport, and also he wanted to let the pattern set before he made an intervention. The purpose of the strategic confrontation in Barbie's presence was to subtly change Barbie's attitudes about her mother.

Part of Barbie's values were that she viewed food as she were undeserving of it; as if she deserved only punishment. Therefore, Erickson did not prescribe food for its nutritional value. Rather, he prescribed food as a punishment. Barbie accepted the intervention because it was in keeping with her own value system. However, while her mind could think of the food as if it were a punishment, her body would accept it as nutrition.

Erickson used the interspersal technique (Erickson, 1966) to elicit internal associations. In his stories, he interspersed the concept of food in conjunction with different social settings. He wanted Barbie to build up a sufficient supply of good associations so that she would begin replacing patterns that were maladaptive. Food would no longer be aversive or viewed as a punishment. Change would happen because Barbie took control of the situation. She was not directly told when or how to change her anorexia. In some of the interventions, she was given extra room to make her own choices. However, this was an "illusion of alternatives." Barbie made choices within the confines of sets that Erickson established, and the sets consisted only of items that were therapeutically beneficial. Also, because she valued being a "good girl," she was obligated to keep her promises and submit to "punishment."

Erickson's intervention of prescribing the mouthwash was carefully seeded and presented in steps. Again, he got Barbie to agree to something that fit with her value system. It was perfectly fine to put cod liver oil in her mouth as long as she didn't swallow it. However, she could not realize the strategic implication of Erickson's prescription. He was disrupting her rigid attitudes and beginning to control what went into her mouth.

Erickson worked to change Barbie's social role. She was a Victim but did not admit to being in the Victim role. Erickson put her in the Persecutor and Rescuer roles (Karpman, 1968) by having her concentrate on her mother's "eating problem."

Therapy was conducted with the family. However, Erickson did not meet with the family as a whole; he met with them individually. It is possible that Barbie was playing out an exaggerated parody of her parent's concern about their own weight. Therefore, Erickson chided the father about his own attitude about eating.

There is a certain kind of passivity inherent in anorexia problems, and Barbie's brothers and sisters were chided out of their own passivity. They could no longer deprive their sister of her *constitutional* rights. (The choice of the word *constitutional* was an intentional double entendre. Erickson was not merely referring to Barbie's legal rights; he was also referring to her physique.)

Erickson was pleased with the gifts and letters Barbie sent. They continued to correspond until Erickson's death in 1980. In each of her letters Barbie made an indirect reference to food. She also gave him an apple doll and sent him flowers made of bread dough. I believe that Erickson would consider Barbie's letters and gifts "proof" that his methods had been effective. Her unwitting communications were on the same level with his own many indirect references to food.

The case has been a success. Through the years, Mrs. Erickson has kept in contact with Barbie, and she is adjusting well personally and socially.

In both the case of Joe and the case of Barbie, Erickson used the utilization method. Moreover, he decided the treatment goals rather than clearly delineating a therapeutic contract with the patient. Especially in the case of Barbie, Erickson worked to promote change in areas where he was uninvited, as for example in the social sphere. It was characteristic of his approach that you might not get half of what you asked for but you could get twice what you bargained for.

The way in which Erickson handled Barbie's refusal to accept "gifts" preserved her autonomy. She did not have to partake of the gifts, merely to accept them. Because it fit her value system, she could not deny that it was right to accept a gift. However, accepting is a positive step toward eating, and again, any minimal strategic change constitutes psychotherapy. Note that Erickson's confrontation of Barbie and her siblings was not about food; it was about "gifts." Food per se was deemphasized and presented in a different light, as a "present."

# CHAPTER 3

# Experiences with Erickson: Personal Therapy, Supervision, Cases Reported by Former Patients, and Cases Observed

## INTRODUCTION

Within the contexts of personal therapy and professional supervision, Milton H. Erickson, M.D., helped me develop into a more positive and effective person and therapist. In this essay, I will present some of my more memorable experiences with Dr. Erickson—experiences that portray him both as a person and as a therapist. I will also relate some experiences reported to me by Erickson's former patients and students. Too often Erickson is thought of as a brilliant technician. One of the purposes of these vignettes is to portray Erickson as I perceived him—a remarkable human being first, and a master therapist second.

Jay Haley (1982, p. 5) remarked that hardly a day went by when he did not use something that he had learned from Erickson. In my case, the measure is hardly an hour! There are several outstanding aspects of Erickson's method that account for my enthusiasm. These aspects will be apparent in the cases that follow. Erickson's approach to teaching, supervision, and therapy was based on common sense. He would often present a simple, common-sense remedy with sufficient drama to make his advice come alive. Also, he would individualize the delivery of his message so that the listener could more easily understand and respond to the instructions contained therein. Finally, Erickson would often mobilize responsiveness indirectly. For example, he would often couch his commonsense advice in an analogy or an anecdote. By this means Erickson could stay "one-step removed," which will be seen to be an important ingredient in effective therapeutic communication.

Erickson's ability to individualize the delivery of his messages was based on his perceptiveness of minimal cues. He attended to the very things that people generally learn to ignore. For example, human beings often delete aspects of sensory experience—steady state information in particular. The human perceptual system is a great "mismatch detector" and notices what is *wrong* in a given situation. In contrast, Erickson trained himself to attend to what is *right*, to pick up on the minimal cues that depict a patient's strengths. He knew that it is easier to promote change by building upon what patients do right rather than by analyzing what they have done wrong.

I do not believe there was anything exceptionally profound about Erickson's advice. But, as will be seen, his *approach* was profound in that he consistently made use of the obvious. Unfortunately, many therapists are so absorbed in their dynamic formulations that they overlook the obvious. However, Erickson watched for the obvious and then presented it back to patients so that they could respond therapeutically in their own way.

## UTILIZING CONTEXTS AND INJUNCTIONS

A hallmark of Erickson's approach was his ability to utilize context. Manipulation of the context, and/or the patient's response to context, can create therapeutic change. Erickson looked for things in the immediate reality situation that could be used therapeutically, often setting up situations where people would spontaneously realize their previously unrecognized abilities to change (Zeig, 1980a; Dammann, 1982).

His therapy was not limited to interpersonal exchange and psychological archaeology. *Erickson understood that change occurs in a context that includes effective communication and that effective communication utilizes context.*

Another aspect of Erickson's approach was that he was sensitively attuned to his environment. He seemed to be always working to influence, to have an effect on others. Perhaps he seemed so alert because he was extraordinarily aware of the injunctive aspect of communication.

As discussed in Chapter 1, Watzlawick (1985) indicated that communication is both indicative and injunctive, that denotation and connotation are present in every communication. Communication is indicative in that facts are reported. The injunctive part of the communication is usually a more covert message that says, "Do something!" It is the injunctive aspect of communication that promotes change.

To illustrate what is meant by "indicative" and "injunctive," consider Erickson's early learning set hypnotic induction. The surface indication is a story about how children approach the task of writing: "When you first learned to write the letters of the alphabet, it was an awfully difficult task. Did you dot the 't' and cross the 'i'? How many bumps are there in an 'n' and an 'm'?"

There is more to this communication than the indicative aspect. There are also numerous injunctions in these two sentences. The overall injunction is, "Go into a trance." Another injunction is, "This task (trance) will be difficult but you can eventually do it automatically." The patient is prodded to "be confused" by the reference to crossing the "i" and dotting the "t." Additionally, the patient is directed to remember things from the past. The last sentence, by changing from past to present tense, also tells a patient to "be absorbed in the memory."

It is not so much a therapist's words or data that promote change.

Change most often comes when patients respond to the therapist's injunctions, having heard what the therapist indirectly tells them to do. More than any other communicator I have ever met, Erickson knew this and was keenly alert to the command aspect of communication.

Context is also part of communication and can be used injunctively. An example of Erickson's use of context arose in one of my first visits to him. At that time, Erickson was not so well known in wider psychological circles. *Uncommon Therapy* (Haley, 1973), the book that put Erickson in the limelight, had just been published.

After a few visits, I decided to videotape Erickson and so I brought my friend, Paul, to Phoenix. Paul was skilled in the use of videotape equipment and we wanted to make videos of Erickson at work because so few existed.

We set up the equipment and recorded Erickson performing a remarkable induction using Paul as a subject. Erickson was working with this individual who had no experience with hypnosis; he directed his efforts toward increasing both Paul's responsiveness and his ability to develop various hypnotic phenomena.

Unfortunately, I would not have the opportunity to enjoy it a second time; the tape was flawed. Paul had forgotten to plug the microphone into the videodeck, so we had a silent tape. As you can see from my wording, I blamed Paul and was more than a bit perturbed at him. I was quite possessive of my time with Erickson. Here I was sharing that time and the video was unusable.

The three of us discussed the problem that evening and Erickson would not let me continue to blame Paul. He pointed out that I was equally responsible for the failure. I acknowledged his point. However, secretly, I felt that he was wrong. I told myself that even Milton Erickson could make a sophomoric mistake! He did not seem to realize that a precious videotape was irretrievably lost; the taping was useless. However, unbeknownst to me, Erickson was going to make use of that silent tape.

The next day, when Paul and I were in Erickson's office, Erickson said to me, "Put on that silent tape." Then he looked at Paul expectantly. At the time, Paul was seated in the patient's chair. Paul looked at the video briefly and then he spontaneously went into a trance! Erickson had used that silent videotape as an induction technique!

A common induction technique is to get a patient to remember a previous hypnotic experience and then access it. When Paul saw the trance that he had been in the day before, he went into a new trance. It didn't matter to him that there was no sound on the tape. Paul was sensitive to the situation. He intuited Erickson's intent and responded accordingly.

I got busy and set up the equipment so that we could tape this day's induction. While still in a trance, Paul got out of his chair and with his right hand cataleptic against his side (he was right-handed) walked to the videotape equipment and checked the sound plug, using only his left hand. He was oblivious both to his surroundings and to the fact that his right arm was cataleptic. After returning to his seat, Paul looked up at Erickson and slowly and mechanically said, "I would like you to teach me more things while I am in this state."

Erickson thought that Paul's catalepsy was a fine example of lateralized behavior. He then underscored that were it not for the silent tape, we would never have had this excellent learning experience.

This incident is but one example of how Erickson used the context. He established Paul's trance by merely manipulating the reality situation and communicating "one-step removed," thereby creating an injunction to which Paul responded. And, characteristically, he did it in a way that accentuated the positive; the "obviously useless" videotape turned out to be valuable!

Incidentally, that second induction is one of the few times when I saw Erickson miss something. As it turned out, Paul was quite responsive to Erickson's minimal cues. During the induction, Erickson looked to me and said something like, "I can't see exactly what is happening, but his blink reflex is altered." While Erickson was talking, Paul's eyes closed.

Later Erickson asked me when and why Paul closed his eyes. I didn't know. Erickson explained that Paul closed his eyes at the reference to the altered blink reflex. But in viewing the videotape, Paul and I realized Erickson was wrong. Actually, when Erickson said, "I can't see . . . ," Paul was so attuned to minimal cues that he took the message literally and quickly shut his eyes. Literalism as evidenced by pinpoint responsiveness to injunctions is often a characteristic of good hypnotic subjects. Paul had heard *"I can't see"* as the injunction *"Eye can't see,"* and responded precisely.

Here are other examples of Erickson's use of context:

*Example One*

Erickson didn't charge me for his time and I wanted to give him a gift to express my appreciation. I didn't have enough money to afford extensive training at that time and it was his style not to charge if patients or students couldn't afford it.

Erickson loved wood carvings; he had an extensive collection of ironwood carvings made by the Seri Indians who live in the desert of northwest Mexico. So I gave Erickson a wood carving, one with an unfinished driftwood base. The top of the carving was a finished duck's head. When I presented the gift to Erickson, he looked at the driftwood and looked at me. He looked at the driftwood, and looked at me. He looked at the driftwood, and looked at me. Then he said, "Emerging."

*Example Two*

A number of years later, the Christmas before he died, Erickson gave me a present of an ironwood owl. I thanked him by saying, "Very wise gift, Dr. Erickson." His symbolism was not lost.

*Example Three*

After the completion of a session in 1974, Erickson was in his wheelchair struggling to surmount the small ramp from the patio to the main house. I rushed over to help him, really wanting to be of service, but he refused my assistance, saying pointedly, "One has to use his own strengths because he knows what he is dealing with." Then he proceeded to push himself into the house. He saw an opportunity to instruct me and he seized upon it.

*Example Four*

In two instances that I know of, Erickson "accidentally" left his patient's file folder open on his desk so that the patients could sneak a look. His notes were usually sparse. On both occasions they read, "Doing well!"

*Example Five*

I felt he even used telephone calls in a directed fashion. He often would answer the phone himself during the training sessions that were held in his office. Then he would continue his train of thought exactly where he left off. Coming back to a departure point in this manner is a technique called structured amnesia (Erickson & Rossi, 1974, p. 229) that is meant to effect a loss of immediate memory for the intervening sequence. It seemed to me that the purpose of taking the call during a session was to make a point to the person in his office, perhaps demonstrating to the patient or student his or her own capacity for amnesia. (Note: Erickson used this technique only in his Hayward Street office which he occupied for the last 10 years of his life. He had no telephone in the room he used in the Cypress Street office he occupied from 1949 to 1969.)

*Example Six*

Erickson also conducted psychotherapy through individualized autographs he inscribed in books. Each autograph was tailored to the recipient and many had a therapeutic intent. Some of the memorable ones he wrote for me were: 1) *"Into each life some confusion should come . . . also some enlightenment."* Erickson made a twist on a famous line from Wordsworth that his mother often quoted. My initial contact with him was bewildering and it was comforting to know there was a possibility that enlightenment could follow. 2) *"Around each corner should be the unexpected."* A rather nice admonition for someone who had tendencies to be overly reliant on conscious planning. 3) *"One of the wonders of the world is the opening of the eyes."* Not bad advice for someone who is primarily auditory. 4) *"Just another book to curl your hair.*" Erickson knew that I valued having curly hair and it was characteristic of him to "hook" his therapy to what the patient/student already valued. 5) Erickson wrote the Foreword to *Change* by Watzlawick, Weakland, and Fisch. He inscribed it, *"May 1974. To Jeff Zeig, Look back in ten years and notice the changes."* This was helpful, sage advice for someone who was in a hurry to achieve mastery. I felt that he was trying to foster in me an appreciation of developmental processes.

Obviously, Erickson did not limit his psychotherapy to verbal comments in the office. He was constantly working, striving to maximize his impact. Erickson was extraordinarily aware of the effect of his communication. He seemed to thrive on finding new opportunities to create influence communication by using aspects of the environment. In addition to utilizing context, he also used other forms of indirection.

## UTILIZING INDIRECTION

A common aspect of Erickson's approach was his use of indirection. Although he could be quite direct, characteristically he was indirect. Paradoxically, indirection is often the most direct method to promote change.

One way Erickson was indirect was that he structured stories to have effects on multiple levels. In a teaching situation, his anecdotes were not only interesting examples of good psychotherapy, but often relevant on other psychological levels.

For example, Paul and I and another student were in Phoenix to learn from Erickson. The three of us were unconsciously vying for Erickson's attention, and of course he noticed. He abruptly changed his train of thought and told us a story about a competitive fellow from the East who came to see him and wanted to go into a trance (see Rosen, 1982a, p. 81, for a complete case description). Erickson used an arm levitation technique and said, "Okay. Now see which hand rises fastest."

One of us asked whether the story was intended to make reference to the competition between us. Erickson acknowledged that he felt the competition and remarked, "I certainly did not want there to be any competition directed toward me." Thereby he implied that the competition could be redirected.

And thus he commented and empathized indirectly. He did not often empathize in the Rogerian sense. He would not have said, "It seems that you are feeling a need to compete." Instead, his story spoke to the idea of competition and to the idea of redirecting it.

When he told his anecdote, we had not yet recognized the feeling of competing but we picked up on his cue. When we directly talked with him about the idea of our competing, he was perfectly willing to discuss the situation openly. His style did not require that issues had to remain at an unconscious level.

Politeness was one reason he didn't bring up the idea of competition directly. He responded with the same level of experience that he was being presented with. Had we openly talked about competition, I think he would have, too. But he believed in the integrity of the unconscious and in being courteous to the unconscious mind. It seemed he followed the dictum that if things are expressed unconsciously, respond accordingly; if things are expressed consciously, discuss them directly.

## Indirection Through Writing

Erickson could also be indirect in his written communication. My initial introduction to him provides an example.

Like so many others, my introduction to Ericksonian thought was through Haley. I read *Advanced Techniques of Hypnosis and Therapy* (Haley, 1967) and was impressed by Erickson's perspective. Subsequently, on a whim, I wrote a letter to my cousin, Ellen, who was studying nursing in Tucson, Arizona, and said, "If you ever get to Phoenix, visit Milton Erickson. The man is a genius."

Ellen responded, "Remember my old roommate, Roxanna Erickson?" They had lived together in San Francisco and I had visited them a few years earlier. At the time Ellen whispered to me that Roxanna's father was a famous psychiatrist. However, I didn't ask her surname and it wouldn't have meant much to me.

So I wrote to Erickson and to Roxanna and asked if I could come to Phoenix to learn and see him work with patients.

Here are excerpts of his letter of November 9, 1973:

> Dear Mr. Zeig:
> I am very flattered by your letter and while I would be
> glad to meet you, the one or two patients I see a day would
> not be worth your while, nor could I use them for your
> instruction. Also, my general state of physical well-being is
> sufficiently rocky so that I am not able to promise an hour
> a day two days in succession.
> I would like to suggest to you that in the reading of my
> works you pay attention to interpersonal relationships, in-
> trapersonal relationships, and the snowballing effect of a
> change in behavior. . . .
> One other matter that I would like to emphasize with you
> is that you recognize that patter, verbiage, directions or sug-
> gestions are awfully unimportant. The really important thing
> is motivation for change and the realization that no one
> person ever knows his true capabilities.
>
> > Sincerely,
> > Milton H. Erickson, M.D.

I was struck by Erickson's comments, and amazed that this important man would take the time to personalize a reply. I wasn't an
especially assertive person, but the letter intrigued me. I wrote that
I understood that he was ill but that I would be grateful for any time
he could spend with me. Then Erickson set up a time for me to visit.

A couple of years later, I mused about Erickson's initial communication. He was ambiguous about the idea of my coming to Phoenix;
it was necessary that I respond a second time. Erickson only took me
as a student after I showed "the really important thing," namely,
motivation!

### USING ANECDOTES TO MAKE THINGS MEMORABLE

Erickson's anecdotes made simple ideas come alive. Not only are
concepts more memorable when presented in story form (Zeig, 1980a,
p. 26), but anecdotes energize the therapeutic situation. I learned this
from Erickson because he helped me change my own life with his
stories.

In 1978, I moved to Phoenix. Occasionally I consulted with Erickson about my own professional or personal difficulties. I once told him I was troubled by a nervous habit of self-consciously smiling at inappropriate times. In response, he told me a story about his hands. He said that as a child he smashed the forefinger of his right hand and damaged the nail. Thereafter, when he went to pick up something valuable, he would pick it up without using his forefinger. But if it were something *not* valuable, he would pick it up using his forefinger. Erickson told me that he had a female student who knew about this habit. Once, this woman handed him her "diamond" engagement ring. Erickson looked at the ring and from the corner of his eye saw the woman had flushed. Then he looked down at his hand and realized that he was holding the ring using his forefinger. (In other words, the ring was not a real diamond and she knew it.)

That was the essence of Erickson's advice to me. I left his office confused. When I thought about it, I realized that the discussion of the diamond ring was analogically saying that my problem wasn't real. It wasn't a bona fide thing! I began to think about the etiology of my "problem," possibly because Erickson had talked about the etiology of his own pattern. At any rate, the therapy worked. I quit smiling self-consciously.

Erickson's anecdotes helped me again and again. On one occasion early in my training, I told Erickson I was afraid of trance. He asked why and I explained, "I don't know. Maybe I'm afraid of blacking out."

Erickson said that he would give me a few examples. He told me about a boy who went hunting with his father. The boy enjoyed deer hunting until the age of 16, when the father announced the son was old enough to go out on his own. The boy was given a gun and he shot a deer. His unexpected reaction was to tremble and go white.

Next Erickson told a story about a beauty contest. He said that the winner of the Miss America Pageant cries and trembles. Then he talked about giving birth. He told of a woman who was afraid of delivery even though she realized that throughout history women easily accomplished the process. Subsequently, Erickson explained to me that I had been in and out of a trance during the session on the previous day.

I then told him I wanted "an anchor experience" so that I could understand how to use hypnosis. He told me two more stories.

The first was about a baseball player who missed the ball when he "anchored" himself. The second was about a medical student who repeated his first year of medical school seven times. When asked what the deltoids were, he would recite verbatim from page one of the textbook. He went back to page one because he needed to anchor himself.

Erickson then looked at me and said, "You want to be able to use hypnosis for various periods of time. You go in and out by letting it happen." The effect of these stories was to produce an enhanced ability to utilize my hypnotic abilities; no longer was I afraid of an untoward reaction from hypnosis.

Anecdotes of this sort are easily interpretable. Basically, Erickson was redefining my fear of "blacking out" and allowing me to accept that part of the initial process of learning may include unexpected emotions. In essence, this technique of redefinition allowed for a more positive interpretation of "blacking out" (i.e., similar feelings can occur after a triumph), and a negative interpretation of the need for an "anchor." But when one overanalyzes stories, often the gestalt is lost. The total is more than the sum of the parts.

Erickson's anecdotes helped me on another occasion. When I moved to Phoenix in July of 1978, my father had a coronary. My mother couldn't get in touch with me because I had just arrived in Phoenix and didn't have a permanent residence, so she sent a telegram to the Ericksons.

When I went to get the telegram, Erickson told me a story about his father, which I will paraphrase as I remember it. It is reported in detail by Rosen (1982a, p. 167).

Erickson said that his father had his first coronary when he was about 80. His father woke up in a small-town hospital in Wisconsin and looked up at the doctor, who told him, "Mr. Erickson, you had a serious coronary. You are going to be in the hospital for a couple of months." Mr. Erickson replied, "I don't have a couple of months. I'll be out of here in a week." A week later, he was out of the hospital.

A few years went by and Mr. Erickson had another coronary. He woke up in the hospital, saw the same doctor, groaned, and said, "Not another week."

A number of years later Mr. Erickson had another coronary. When he regained consciousness, he said to the doctor (same doctor), "You know, Doc, I am getting a little older now. I guess I'll have to be in the hospital for two weeks."

In his nineties, Mr. Erickson had another coronary. Upon recovery, he told the doctor, "You know, Doc, I thought that fourth coronary was going to carry me away. But now, I'm starting to lose faith in the fifth."

At the age of 97½, Mr. Erickson was setting out on a ride with his daughters. After getting into the car, he realized he had forgotten his hat and returned to the house for it. After some time, the sisters remarked to each other, "This must be it." In fact, Mr. Erickson *had* died, due to a suspected cerebral hemorrhage. Erickson commented, "He was right to lose faith in the fifth." Then he looked at me and said, "The really important thing is your father's motivation."

I really appreciated Erickson's help, and the drama of the tale made it memorable and effective. I was conflicted about my responsibility to my family and his story placed things in perspective and helped me to decide my course of action. Also, the context should be noted: His intervention was unsolicited; I didn't ask for his assistance. It was Erickson's style that if you were in his presence, he had license to do hypnosis and psychotherapy. To some this might seem unethical and manipulative, but to Erickson it was a matter of social courtesy. He was going to respond to the situation in the most meaningful way possible. The recipient of the communication was free to respond to the extent that he or she wished.

In the story about his father, Erickson indicated his view of the proper attitude people should have in dealing with death and illness. As evidenced by the way he died, he was not hypocritical; he modeled the principles he espoused.

## MODELING HOW TO DIE

On Sunday morning, March 23, 1980, Erickson fell ill from an overpowering infection—perhaps from a ruptured diverticulum. He was semicomatose until Tuesday night at 11:00 p.m., and died with Mrs. Erickson and his daughter, Roxanna, in the room. The time that he hung on provided an opportunity for his family members to fly to Phoenix.

Erickson was somewhat responsive during his time in the hospital, but only to family members. When they spoke to him, he would often flutter his eyelids.

His manner of death was in keeping with his life-style. Erickson was proud of the fact that his father had died while going out to do something, and his own death was similar. Erickson had just completed a week-long seminar, and students had arrived for Monday's seminar. And while he was in the hospital he clearly struggled to stay alive. I got the feeling that he never gave up. He seemed to take every breath he could, and then he took one more.

After his death, we went to the family home for a late dinner. There was no extended mourning. Erickson promoted the idea that life was for the living and that deep grieving was unnecessary.

Erickson often used teasing humor to diffuse feelings about death. Once when I was concerned about his failing health, he misquoted Tennyson and said, "Let there be no moaning at the bar when my ship sets out to sea." He also teased that dying was the last thing he was going to do (cf. Rosen 1982a, p. 170; also Rosen, 1982b, p. 475). His attitude was, "We all start dying when we are born. Some of us are faster than others. Why not live and enjoy, because you can wake up dead. You won't know about it. But someone else will worry then. Until then, live—enjoy life."

On another occasion he intoned, "Do you want a good recipe for longevity? Always be sure to get up in the morning. And you can ensure that by drinking a lot of water before you go to bed" (Zeig, 1980a, p. 269).

Erickson told another group of students that he wanted to be told jokes when he was on his deathbed. Unfortunately, I didn't know of his request until too late.

## MEMORABLE ONE-LINERS AND ANALOGIES

Anecdotes are only one method of making things memorable. Memories can be "tagged" through unusual quips, the turn of a phrase, or by simple analogies. Here are some examples:

When we set up the First International Congress on Ericksonian Approaches to Hypnosis and Psychotherapy, Erickson hypothesized that I would probably become nationally known in hypnosis circles and could become an officer in a professional society. "Do you want to know how to get ahead in an organization?" he queried. "You bet!" I replied. *"Drag* people up with you."

I was at an out-of-town professional meeting where I was treated shabbily and Erickson was seriously slighted. I was surprised at what had transpired and felt badly for Erickson. I reluctantly and with some trepidation called him to tell him about it. He was nonplussed; he chuckled and said, "Welcome to the adult world!"

On occasions he said, "Problems are the roughage of life. And any soldier that has been on K-rations knows how important roughage is in a diet" (cf. Zeig, 1980a, p. 185). Similarly, he proffered, "Make all the happiness you can, the troubles will always find you." Also, "Dealing *adequately* with the good and bad alike is the real joy of living." To another student he intoned, "Psychotherapy begins at home." To a colleague's young daughter, "Does it hurt to be that cute?" To a student, "Happiness is the endowment with value of all the things you have" (Thompson, 1982, p. 418). To a colleague, Marion Moore, "Hypnosis is a vital relationship in one person, stimulated by the warmth of another."

*Indirection Using Analogies*

Once Erickson presented me with a bit of advice in the form of a rather nice analogy. Unfortunately, I have yet to completely master the advice, but I have used the same analogy effectively with some of my patients.

I explained to Erickson that I had been working too hard and asked him for some assistance. He talked with me about his own life. He said that during the years he worked at Eloise Hospital in Michigan, he regretted not taking enough vacations with his family.

Then he gave an example. "When a man sits down for a meal, he might want to have a cocktail. Then he could have an appetizer. After that, he might want to have a palate refresher. Then he might want to have a salad, and then there is the main course, which has meat and some kind of carbohydrate, and a vegetable. After that, there would be a dessert, and then there would be coffee or tea." Then

Erickson looked up at me and said, "Man cannot live by protein alone."

Part of Erickson's mentality was to present ideas by getting one-step removed from the situation. Being *one-step removed* is the essence of indirection.

The advice I needed to hear was, "Don't work too hard." There wasn't really much more that he could say to me but, "Well, don't work so hard." But Erickson gave his advice in terms of an analogy that made the idea memorable and alive.

### Using Words Memorably

Not only did he use anecdotes, analogies, and one-liners to make things memorable, he also used particular words. As was previously mentioned, Erickson studied the dictionary at an early age. Awareness of the multiple meanings of words was a cornerstone of his indirect technique.

In a teaching session he was challenging me with anecdotes to increase my flexibility. Occasionally, he would look up at me and say, "You're rigid." I mused, "OK, compared to Erickson, I'm rigid." Subsequently I thought about this communication. "Rigid" could have referred to my physical posture as well as to my mental set. When people go into trance, their behavior is fixed and rigid. Erickson knew I questioned my ability to enter trance and I believe his confrontation about rigidity was two-pronged.

An excellent example of how Erickson used each word as a tool is contained in his article, "The Method Employed to Formulate a Complex Story for the Induction of the Experimental Neurosis in a Hypnotic Subject" (Erickson, 1944). In it he presents the rationale for each word chosen for the induction.

### Indirection to Guide Associations

Anecdotes, one-liners and analogies do not merely energize the therapy and make ideas memorable; they are also used to guide associations. Problems are often caused by preconscious associations. If problems are generated at the level of associations, it often is at that level that they can be best changed. Anecdotes can be used to help reassociate the patient's internal life. Merely talking about a situation is not necessarily therapeutic.

I remember how Erickson got me to stop smoking a pipe. I was an addicted pipe smoker, and he didn't approve of smoking. On some level, I must have approved. At the time, it fit my image of being "the young psychologist."

Erickson saw me smoking my pipe in his backyard. (I would not smoke inside his office.) When I came in for our session, he told me a long, lighthearted, convoluted story about a friend of his who was a pipe smoker. As I remember it, this friend looked awkward smoking his pipe, and he also looked awkward putting tobacco into the pipe.

I remember thinking, "I've been smoking a pipe for years. I don't look awkward." Erickson continued to tell me how the friend looked awkward: He looked awkward when he tamped the tobacco down; he looked awkward when he lit up the tobacco; he looked awkward because he didn't know where to put his pipe; he looked awkward because he didn't know how to hold the pipe.

I swear this story went on for an hour. I never knew that there were so many different ways that someone could look awkward. All the time I kept thinking to myself, "Why is he telling me this story? I don't look awkward."

Shortly after the session, I left Phoenix to drive back to the San Francisco area where I lived. When I reached California, I said to myself, "I am not smoking anymore." I put away the pipe forever. I got rid of all my expensive pipes and lighters.

I had responded to Erickson's injunction. I certainly didn't want to look awkward in his eyes. Moreover, his technique was a pattern disruption; he attached the idea of awkwardness to pipe smoking. Subsequently, smoking a pipe just didn't seem appealing.

## Indirect Confrontation

Indirect technique can be used to confront as well as to guide. Here are two examples:

Erickson had been a voracious reader, but when his vision failed he watched television. Erickson loved nature shows and often used metaphors from them in his teaching and therapy. I tried to ask him a question once when one of his favorite programs was on. He said that he was confined to the house and that watching these shows was one of the only ways he had to get out. He caught my attention and intoned, "If I miss my nature show, I get angry." I said, "I'm leaving."

Even Erickson's confrontation used indirection. He was simultaneously setting some boundaries, teaching me, and trying to find a unique way to get across his message.

Not long before he died, Erickson asked what I was charging for an hour of therapy; at the time he was charging $40.00 per hour. I replied, "Forty dollars." He said, "Thirty-five?" as if he hadn't heard me. I corrected, "No. Forty dollars." Again, he inquired, "Thirty-five?" I said, "I understand."

It was not that he was incapable of being incisive and directly confrontive. For example, I know of more than one case where Erickson told a mismatched couple to separate. He strived to use the technique that seemed best destined to elicit the desired response.

## SUMMARY

Erickson's therapy was often that of an old-time doctor. He offered a simple, commonsense remedy presented "one-step removed" so that it would come alive and be heard. Thereby, the patient could respond to the injunction. It was not that there was anything especially profound about the advice. It did not seem that Erickson said something extraordinary about human personality. But where most therapists are absorbed in their dynamic formulations, Erickson attended to the obvious and thought out the most effective ways to use it therapeutically.

## DIRECT SUPERVISION

Erickson was an unusual supervisor whose instructions, like his therapy, were based on one-step-removed common sense. His technique as a supervisor was as unique as his technique as a therapist and teacher. Here are some examples:

*Example One*

After Erickson retired from private practice, he referred a number of patients to me. One of these had a peculiar contamination phobia. Whenever he saw white powder on anything, he became phobic about that object forever and would avoid it, to the point where he was terrorizing his acquaintances and family. For example, he once saw white powder on the television, and because he wouldn't touch it, his wife and daughters had to turn the television on and off and change the channels for him.

In the first session with this patient, I got a history and description of the problem. Then I called Erickson and asked him for supervision. He agreed to see me, and so I went to his home and told him about the patient in elaborate detail. I asked how he would handle the problem, and his advice was simple. He stoically said, "Send him to Canada." Then he added, "As a matter of fact, send him to northern Canada."

Erickson told me this type of patient was capable of becoming violent: He could get the idea that someone had intentionally put white powder on an object to contaminate him.

Erickson didn't have anything more to say. I didn't accept the advice about Canada because I didn't have any idea what he had meant, but I was sufficiently wary that I only worked with the patient for one more session. In essence, I gave him a behavioral technique of pattern disruption and told him how to apply it. Because of the man's particular dynamics, I wanted him to depend on himself rather than on my intervention. I told him not to contact me regardless of whether or not the therapy I suggested was successful. I left it all up to him.

Sometime after the therapy, I was musing about Erickson's advice. I finally got it. When Erickson initially gave me his advice about the case, I was too stunned by his brief, impassive reply to immediately realize what he was talking about. Also, when you live in the Phoenix desert area, it is easy to forget about the weather in the northern latitudes. Erickson had been suggesting an in vivo desensitization! I believe that Erickson did not literally mean that I should send the man to Canada. Rather he was directing me to look for contexts in which the problem wouldn't exist. At the same time, he was suggesting that I rely on my own resources, not on his advice.

*Example Two*

Another case that Erickson referred to me was one in which he worked with four generations of a family: He had seen the grandfather, the father, the two sons, and the family of one of the sons. He referred the depressed wife of one of the sons. Erickson told me about the pattern of failure that characterized the men in the family and explained that the husband was rigid, aloof, and emotionally unexpressive. Part of the wife's depression was due to the fact that her husband was emotionally distant.

During the course of the treatment, I consulted with Erickson a number of times. At one point, the woman was going to sell her business. I didn't think this was a good idea and so I asked Erickson about it. He told me to tell her, "Keep the business because it sets a good example for the children." His advice was on target. Although he had seen the wife only once previously, he had ascertained her values. One of the primary things in her life was being a good model for her children.

With subsequent therapy, I helped the wife, but I thought not enough. I discussed the situation with Erickson again. He responded with a story. It was an anecdote about the Seri Indians who made ironwood carvings. Erickson explained that the Seris were poor and had only primitive tools. After a day of fishing they might catch only one or two fish for the tribe. At night, they would walk out into the desert and sleep underneath the stars.

He explained that an anthropologist, who subsequently became a personal friend, visited the Seris. The man interested the Indians in fashioning wood carvings from the ironwood readily available in the Sonoran Desert. Then, the Seris made ironwood carvings of the wild animals they knew. They used no models; the carvings were made from their own memory. They used primitive tools—ocean sand as sandpaper, shoe polish as dye.

The carvings became extremely popular and the Seris became rich. Now they were able to buy fish nets and pickup trucks. Erickson explained that they would throw their fish nets into the ocean and soon they would catch a lot of fish for the tribe. Erickson followed by saying, "And then they would take their pickup trucks and drive out into the desert and sleep underneath the stars."

That was Erickson's advice about this woman. Again, I had to do some processing to get the point, but the message became clear: Even though some people change their circumstances, they may not really change their fundamental attitudes or behaviors.

If Erickson had told me, "You know, some people don't change their fundamental behavior even when their circumstances change," I wouldn't have remembered it. He made his point memorable by weaving it into a dramatic, one-step-removed vignette.

I also conducted some "family therapy" in this case, using a device I had learned from Erickson. He had told me about a technique he used to encourage communication in emotionally distant families. He would tell family members to take turns reading the Ann Landers column from the newspaper. They were to do this each night at the dinner table for one year. The *letters* were to be read, but the *replies* were to be saved until after some family discussion (with the stipulation, of course, that although much of her advice is sound, it may not necessarily be correct, or the only solution, or applicable to the family at the time). Erickson said if you read Ann Landers for a year, you have encountered the whole gamut of human problems.

I've used this technique on a number of occasions. It's an excellent way to guide a family toward more contact and the discussion of moral issues.

## Example Three

I had a difficult schizophrenic patient and I asked Erickson for supervision. Erickson asked if the patient liked music. When he found out the patient was musically inclined, he said, "Well, if the patient plays the piano, have him learn to play a song one note off." Because the patient played the guitar, I had him learn a song one fret off.

The advice was quite sensible because it was symbolic of the actions of schizophrenic patients; they live their lives just a bit off-key. But in order to play a song off-key, one has to learn it correctly first. I often have used variations of this method in my work with schizo-phrenic patients.

*Example Four*

The previously mentioned patient with acute hysterical psychotic episodes (see Chapter One) suffered from occasional auditory hallu-cinations. Erickson told me that I should continue his technique of having her write out everything the voices said. This was a benevolent ordeal (cf. Haley, 1984) that served as an effective pattern disruption.

*Example Five*

I consulted with Erickson about a couple who were in an escalating symmetric relationship fraught with bitterness; each blamed the other for causing problems. He told me about a technique that he had used successfully in a number of cases. In a conjoint session, I was to say to one member of the couple, "You know, in any given situation, your spouse is 60 percent right." Then I was to say to the other, "In any given situation, *your* spouse is 60 percent right." Then I could say to both of them, "You know that adds up to a nice 120 percent."

I followed up by telling the couple, "As soon as your spouse brings up a point of disagreement, point out the 60 percent that is correct. Then, you are free to inform him/her about the 40 percent that can be improved." I explained that this technique emphasized what they were already doing; it really did not add much new. Usually they interspersed what the spouse was doing right when they were making their criticisms. The only change was to consolidate what the other was doing right and present those aspects first.

This technique also can provide effective pattern disruption. The therapist inserts himself into the marital struggle. Thereby, it can be effective even if the couple doesn't complete the task. If a member of the couple just remembers the advice at the moment of conflict, it can diffuse some of the feelings before they get out of hand.

*Example Six*

I inquired about techniques for weight control, a problem that typically has a low success rate. Erickson indicated that it was important to effect a reorientation in attitude. When a patient requested to lose 40 pounds, he switched and talked to them about losing one pound. "How do you climb Squaw Peak?" he asked hypothetically. "One step at a time."

## Example Seven

Although I have already published this (Zeig, 1980a), I will provide some additional details here of one of my favorite cases of supervision.

An attorney contacted Erickson about a case where he believed hypnosis was being used improperly. It was a murder case and the police used hypnosis on the witnesses. The defense attorney asked Erickson if he would testify, but Erickson said he was too old and suggested the attorney call me.

I told the defense attorney that I had never testified in a courtroom before, but I would be glad to render an opinion about whether hypnosis was used properly. The attorney said he would have to submit my credentials to the court before he could use me as an expert witness. He told the court that I was trained by Milton Erickson, the world's foremost authority on hypnosis, and my credentials were accepted.

Subsequently, the prosecuting attorney contacted Erickson, who had taught investigative hypnosis to special officers on the Phoenix police force. In fact, he may have trained the officer who conducted the hypnotic session in this particular case. Erickson told the prosecuting attorney that he couldn't testify because of his infirmity. So the prosecuting attorney asked if he would give a deposition. Erickson agreed.

When the prosecuting attorney submitted Erickson's credentials, he noted, "As the defense has acknowledged that Milton Erickson is the foremost authority on hypnosis, we would like to have him render an opinion in this case." Of course, Erickson was accepted by the court.

So it was Erickson for the prosecution, and Zeig for the defense. Needless to say, I got a little nervous.

I asked Erickson why he had changed his mind and decided to testify, and he said, "You have got a few things to learn, haven't you?" I said, "You bet."

Even though it was difficult for Erickson to travel, he rode the police van to the station to view the videotape. In addition to wanting to instruct me, Erickson must have thought that the case was important.

As we talked, I told Erickson I was nervous about going to court and asked him for some advice. He initiated the following story with the phrase, "Know the opposing attorney."

Erickson explained that he had once testified in a child custody case on behalf of the husband. He believed that the wife was suffering from severe psychological problems and that the husband was the best person to have custody, since it was possible that the wife would be abusive.

Erickson then went on to say that he had suspected the opposing attorney was a very thorough individual. He figured things would be difficult because the husband's attorney did *not* give him any information about the opposition. When the day came for him to give his testimony, the opposing attorney came well prepared; she had 14 typewritten pages of questions for Erickson. She opened with challenging questions: "Dr. Erickson, you say that you're an expert in psychiatry. Who is your authority?" Erickson responded, "I am my *own* authority." He knew that if he named someone, this well-prepared lawyer would begin to undermine his expertise by citing conflicting authorities.

The lawyer then asked, "Dr. Erickson, you say that you are an expert in psychiatry. What is psychiatry?" Erickson said that he provided the following response: "I can give you this example. Anyone who is an expert on American history would know something about Simon Girty, also called 'Dirty Girty.' Anyone who is not an expert on American history would not know about Simon Girty, also called 'Dirty Girty.' Any expert on American history should know about 'Simon Girty,' also called 'Dirty Girty.' "

Erickson explained that when he looked up at the judge, he was sitting with his head buried in his hands. The clerk of the court was underneath the table trying to find his pencil. The husband's lawyer was trying to suppress an uncontrollable laugh.

After Erickson gave that (seemingly irrelevant) example, the lawyer put aside her papers and said, "No further questions, Dr. Erickson."

Then Erickson looked at me and said, "And the lawyer's name . . . was Gertie."

Erickson's anecdote was amusing and engaging, a delightful way to make a point. If Erickson had simply told me, "Don't be intimidated by this situation," the impact would have been minimal. But as a result of his one-step-removed method of communication, it is now impossible for me to go into a courtroom without thinking of "Dirty Girty."

Later, Erickson talked about another technique he used successfully in the courtroom. He said that often the opposing attorney would build emotional momentum and then pose an impassioned question, the inanity of which was obscured by the emotion of the moment.

At this point, Erickson would act a bit dumb. He would say to the judge, "I am sorry. I missed that question. Would you please have the clerk read it back to me?" Erickson said that when the clerk of the court read the question back in a flat voice, it lost all of its dramatic intensity, allowing the jury and everyone else in the court to see how stupid the question really was.

After the case was resolved when the defendant pleaded guilty, we discussed our findings with each other. We agreed that the hypnosis had not been used improperly. In fact, Erickson said that because the officer had used a standardized technique, the hypnosis actually had little effect on the subject; few responses were actually elicited.

## Example Eight

A public figure came to see me with a problem of a personal nature. To ensure confidentiality, he did not give his correct name. When I asked Erickson for some supervision, he insisted that I get his correct name, stating, "Once the unconscious keeps one thing from you, it will keep other things from you."

## Example Nine

During one of my early visits to Phoenix, Erickson asked me to see one of his patients. I was pleased that he had so much faith in me. After seeing the young man, I formulated my impressions in detail and prepared myself for the discussion with Erickson. When he asked me about the case I launched into the man's psychodynamics. He stopped me abruptly and asked me what the patient needed. I was stumped. He replied that all the patient wanted was a big brother to talk to.

Erickson believed that theoretical formulations were a Procrustean bed that limited the practitioner. Each person should be treated as a unique individual. Dynamic formulations are of value to the extent they can be used strategically.

*Example Ten*

I once asked for advice about a difficult borderline patient of years past who was harassing me with phone calls. Erickson suggested that I should tell the patient, "The next time you call, call me at a time I am not home!"

Erickson meant for me to be firm and confrontive with the patient, not to be rude. I didn't follow his advice because I couldn't find a way to make that statement without being sarcastic. However, I was able to use a similar technique in the same situation with another patient.

*Example Eleven*

I told Erickson about a dermatitis patient who scratched himself while sleeping, thereby disrupting both his and his wife's rest. Erickson suggested that the man wrap his fingers with tape one by one before going to bed. I said that it was a long-standing problem. He replied, "Tell him to get a lot of tape."

This benevolent ordeal was successful. Again it was the common-sense advice of an old time doc.

*Example Twelve*

I asked about a case where there was the possibility of the father having a detrimental effect on his young child. The wife was not about to leave and she did not seem able to intervene. Erickson told me about a technique he used successfully which involved telling the husband that he couldn't expect to understand his child until he was a teen and they could really talk. Up to that point, child rearing was really his wife's job. He told me that it might keep the father distant, and by the time the teen years arrived there would be enough personality development to provide sufficient insulation.

## Minimal Cues

Erickson's use of minimal cues was remarkable. He would pick up on subtle changes and use them therapeutically and diagnostically. Rosen (1982b, p. 467) pointed out that Erickson learned to recognize the typing patterns of his secretaries and could tell if they were premenstrual, menstrual, or postmenstrual (see also Zeig, 1980a, p. 162). Haley (1982, p. 13) discussed how Erickson recognized a woman's newly discovered pregnancy by the change in color of her forehead. (Ed. note: Chloasma is the medical term for facial discoloration associated with pregnancy, usually either across the forehead or on the nose and cheeks. It can be a very discrete discoloration, particularly in early pregnancy. However, it often goes unnoticed by all but the most astute observer.)

Sometimes Erickson would make his observations known to patients. In one case, he discerned patterned behavior when a husband was lying. He told the wife about it and in a conjoint session allowed her to ask the husband questions that would uncover the lies.

Erickson also utilized minimal cues to work on subtle levels. Often he would tell stories by directing his voice to the floor and unobtrusively observing people's reactions out of his peripheral vision. The effect of this technique was that patients could perceive his voice as internal dialogue. Also, when talking to a group, he could change the locus of his voice to mark out a message for a particular person.

Also, Erickson did not increase his voice tone when there were traffic sounds outside his office. Most speakers raise their voice and thereby inadvertently cue their listeners to the traffic sounds. By not increasing his voice tone, he encouraged those to whom he was talking to remain unaware of a disturbing sound—a reaction akin to the classic hypnotic phenomenon of negative hallucination (Zeig, 1985a, p. 328).

Because Erickson emphasized observation in his work, part of his training approach was directed to enhancing my own perceptiveness. He used a number of techniques, including telling intriguing stories about observation and challenging me to conduct my own experiments. For example, I was told to watch children in a playground and anticipate whom they would play with, what they would do next, etc. Also, I was to watch a group in action and diagnose which person was going to leave first, who would speak next, etc.

In response to a request for methods to improve my ability to read minimal cues, he noted that observing is like learning the alphabet. "You learn it early, then accumulate new usage." He asked me what "zyzzva" meant. When I asked, he said, "Look it up." Erickson was saying that there is no easy way to learn to use minimal cues. It is a matter of practice and experience.

In the same session, he told me a story about a woman who moved her fists across her chest to the opposite shoulder. He said this mannerism could mean she had a lump in her breast and didn't want to admit it, or that she was a small-breasted woman and that she didn't like it. He indicated that in this instance the fist was an angry gesture. (I reflected on what my nonverbal communication was that day.)

Erickson told about going to a mentalist with a friend to demonstrate to the friend that the mentalist could give correct answers but that it had nothing to do with ESP. It was amazing how perceptive the mentalist was. Subsequently, Erickson showed the friend a set of fictitious answers that he had written out prior to the visit. Actually, the person was not a mentalist at all, he was just good at reading minimal cues and subvocal speech. Erickson "thought" the fictitious answers when questioned and the mentalist was able to read his nonverbal behavior (Rosen, 1982a, p.192).

Erickson related a vignette about a famous expert on nonverbal behavior. During a visit, Erickson saw a piece of sculpture on the man's mantel and admired it. Throughout the conversation, Erickson avoided looking at that artwork because he didn't want the expert to see how much he coveted it. Their conversation concluded, Erickson said the man thanked him for the visit and said, "And, yes, you can have the sculpture!"

On another occasion, Erickson explained to me that an expert on accents might be able to determine much about a person's upbringing. Words learned in grade school might reflect a particular regional accent. If the person subsequently moved to a different area of the country, high school vocabulary could have a different accent. Spoken concepts learned in college might indicate where in the country the person studied.

When training his residents, he would have them take a patient's pulse manually. Erickson would sit across the room and get a reading by observation, perhaps noting the pulse beats in the patient's neck. He told examples of his students missing the fact that a patient had an artificial limb or an artificial eye, and admonished them to note on initial contact if the patient had two eyes, two ears, two arms, two legs, five fingers on each hand, etc.

He said he could tell half a block away whether a driver would turn his car to the left or to the right because, unbeknownst to himself, the driver would signal his intentions, often by shifting his body away from the direction of the turn. This is an example of ideomotor signals. When we think of a behavior, we often act it out minimally and subconsciously. Erickson was an expert at reading and utilizing ideomotor behavior. Most people overlook minimal cues out of ignorance, lack of training, preoccupation, or because they think that not much information is contained in them.

## Summary

Erickson's case supervision with me was brief and problem-oriented. He was interested in eliciting my potentials as a therapist, not in forcefeeding information. He would turn matters back to me, thereby encouraging self-reliance.

Erickson's commonsense supervision was similar to his therapy and teaching. Unlike other supervisors, he was not interested in doing his own therapy through me. Rather, he was interested in seeing that I develop my own style and my own methods.

## REPORTED THERAPIES

I have seen a number of Erickson's previous patients and asked them about their therapy. Invariably, there was a unique aspect to their reports that sheds light on the Ericksonian approach. In a number of these reports Erickson was unsuccessful or had partial success. However, the interventions are still interesting to study.

## Example One

I helped a patient stop smoking. Years before, he had unsuccessfully seen Erickson to stop smoking, noting, "Erickson told me that I wasn't going to stop smoking and, in fact, I didn't." On the same occasion he talked with Erickson about his anxiety in social situations. Erickson told him stories and suggested that when he went into a room full of people, he should think to himself, "Don't give a damn; don't give a damn; don't give a damn." The patient said, "I have used that technique to this day, and it works. I seem to feel better when I walk into a room."

## Example Two

An ambulatory psychotic patient requested hypnosis to help him accomplish some bizarre schemes for changing the world. Years before he had similarly consulted with Erickson, who had told him, "I can't hypnotize you because you've got such quick eye movements." The patient had accepted the reply.

Erickson's reply was a tangential and indirect reference to the man's paranoia, energy, and hypervigilance. In keeping with his style of indirection, he was not confrontive. Because Erickson did not follow up with the man, I assume he thought that the man could not be helped.

## Example Three

A female acquaintance consulted with Erickson about weight control. The therapy consisted of advice and anecdotes and the results seemed positive.

Erickson tried to create an aversive attitude to overeating by indicating, "It is disguised suicide, an attempt to punish yourself for something you don't have, or haven't done." An ordeal was suggested which involved climbing Squaw Peak ten times for each pound gained (I don't believe Erickson expected the patient to do this; it was probably pattern disruption. If she thought about the task, even preconsciously, it might prevent overeating.) She was further confronted to make a list of her food intake to see what she really ate. "Do you enjoy lying to yourself?" Erickson inquired. When she reported eating to "fill holes" in her life, he reminded her that she should fill holes with appropriate things.

Stories were told to reinforce the advice. For example, one of the Erickson children saw some birthday cake, went out and ran a mile, came back and ate the cake. The calories expended equalled the calories consumed. After eating the cake, she said, "It wasn't worth it." Erickson also suggested attitude change by discussing a patient who changed his tastes and started enjoying vegetables.

*Example Four*

A friend of mine and a fellow psychologist attended one of Erickson's teaching seminars. When it was over, Erickson singled him out and invited him into the main house. My friend felt honored.

During the discussion that ensued, Erickson asked Mrs. Erickson to bring out a tie the family had bought for him. Of course it was purple. For a half hour he and Erickson discussed the tie: how the threads fit together, the stains that added character, the wrinkles, and the aging. The sun was setting and the whole experience was emotional in ways my friend didn't fully comprehend.

After some time, there was a delayed *aha!* Erickson was discussing aspects of family ties!

Again, something was taken out of the reality situation and used symbolically and metaphorically. Erickson's perceptiveness was also evident. The man reported that the topics were really relevant to his immediate situation.

*Example Five*

One patient explained that on an initial visit she found herself getting sleepy and bored while listening to Erickson, and she became embarrassed. Then she realized that was what Erickson wanted, so she closed her eyes and went into a trance (Zeig, 1980a, p. 18). Another student asked Erickson for hypnosis but was informed that because of his overly vigilant style Erickson would have to spend hours telling him shaggy dog stories and bore him into a trance. Almost any behavior can be used therapeutically, or as an induction, even boredom. Although on the surface boredom seems antithetical to good therapy, Erickson made use of it and showed that it could be a powerful and valuable technique.

*Example Six*

A man requested treatment for smoking and was seen for one session. The patient was homosexual but didn't want to make that fact public. To effect therapy, Erickson used that particular value. He informed the man that he gave away his sexual orientation by the way he behaved when he smoked. He also gave him some other therapy for smoking including some behavioral techniques; Erickson gave him a number of tasks to keep his hands busy. However, the therapy was ineffective. The man's rationalization was that Erickson made it so easy to stop that he decided he didn't need to try.

*Example Seven*

Certainly, many of Erickson's instructions fell on deaf ears. One of my patients said her husband had seen Erickson years before for weight control but never lost weight. The husband quit treatment after being told that he would never lose weight until he resolved things with his mother. The family secretly agreed with Erickson. It is interesting to note that Erickson used a psychodynamic interpretation in this case. He was not opposed to such methods out of hand.

*Example Eight*

A rather aloof man who did not have much emotional range and had low self-esteem consulted me for hypnosis. It also happened that he was homosexual. He had consulted with Erickson and said he was impressed but afraid of him, so he had trouble being open. Even though the patient never felt at ease, his problems gradually improved.

The patient remembered that Erickson interpreted a dream. I thought that was interesting because I didn't know that Erickson interpreted dreams, so I asked to hear more. The patient replied, "Well, the dream was about an animal, a marmot, and Erickson said it was about my mother. When I asked why, he said, Well, "ma" is the first two letters of Ma, and "mar" stands for Ma, and "mot" is the first three letters of mother. So the dream is about your mother." The man said that at the time he thought, "My god, I never knew that my unconscious mind was so creative."

Erickson might have thought that it was beneficial for this man to do some thinking about his mother, so he found a way to move things in that direction. In the process he did some remarkable ego building.

## PREDICTIONS

Erickson challenged his students to develop an ability to predict behavior and use predictions diagnostically as well as therapeutically. For example, he gave me the novel *Nightmare Alley* by William Gresham and told me to read the first page and tell him what it said on the last page (personal communication, 1974). I couldn't do it, but when I finished the book I realized the ending was clearly indicated on the first page. He also told students to read books both forward and backward and predict what would happen in the ensuing or preceding chapter (Zeig, 1980a, p. 128). Understanding how behavior is unconsciously patterned can help a therapist be more effective.

To create powerful interventions, Erickson used his perceptiveness of minimal cues and his acquired knowledge of how the patient's social history was an influential determinant. I have seen patients of Erickson's who were surprised by the accuracy of his predictions.

### Example One

One woman came to Erickson as a student. He asked her to write down the customary information that he requested of all new patients and students—present date, name, address, telephone, marital status, number of children (names and ages), occupation, education (including degrees and universities attended), age, birthdate, number of brothers and sisters (names and ages), and whether the person's formative years were spent in an urban or rural environment.

Erickson interrupted her writing and said, "You are European." She confirmed this but did not think very much of his observation. There is quite a difference between the script of someone who learned to write in Europe and that of someone who learned to write in the United States.

Then Erickson said, "You are probably southern European, either from Italy or Greece." She thought that was not unusually perceptive; her coloring indicated her background.

Subsequently, Erickson shifted into high gear. He said, "And you were fat when you were a child." The patient was floored; at the time of her visit she was quite thin. She asked Erickson how he knew. He explained that she held herself the way a fat person does.

Erickson's incisive interventions had a number of effects. He took control of the relationship and broke the patient out of any preconceived set that she might have attempted to establish. Moreover, he established his credibility as a diagnostician and observer. He meticulously trained himself to attend to minute details and use that information to predict sequences of behavior.

*Example Two*

One of Erickson's former patients consulted me after Erickson died. I asked her if she remembered any special experiences with Erickson. She said that during the initial interview, Erickson had looked up at her and said, "You were not your mother's favorite." She was a little shocked and replied affirmatively.

Erickson then said, "You were your grandmother's favorite, probably your maternal grandmother." Again he was right. The patient was surprised at his perceptiveness and impressed with his acumen. Again, Erickson made good use of his diligent self-training and attentiveness to minimal cues.

*Example Three*

One of Erickson's former patients sought me out for therapy. Two decades previously, shortly after she married, she had suffered from fainting spells. Medical tests showed nothing and she consulted Erickson, who saw her and her spouse. Erickson thought that she was not properly matched; her husband was a cold and distant individual. In the patient's presence, Erickson confronted the man without effect. Then he suggested to the patient that she divorce, but she adamantly refused. Then, recognizing that she would be a good mother, Erickson suggested that she have children! She agreed and therapy was successfully terminated after a few months, with the admonition that when she reached her forties she would probably need more therapy.

In her early forties, this patient called Erickson because she was again fainting. Erickson had died and Mrs. Erickson referred her to me. The patient had reached a developmental milestone of adult life. Both of her children had turned out well and enrolled in college. She no longer had a constructive organizing force in her life (her children had served that purpose), and her fainting spells returned.

Interpreting her struggles to maintain her balance and stand independently on her own two feet would not have effected change. Neither Erickson nor I confronted her in that manner.

Erickson's intervention had kept the patient out of treatment for 20 years. His style was to achieve symptom control or help a person surmount a developmental problem, then send the patient out to live his/her own life. As a pragmatic therapist, he would not try to accomplish long-term character change unless he thought it was really necessary.

## Example Four

I had an idea for a research project involving visual perception, so I asked Erickson to work with Paul to hypnotically induce differential color vision out of each eye. However, he was unable to get the effect.

After the session, Paul took a walk and returned with a gallon of milk and a large amount of milk chocolate. Paul's purchase was surprising; we were leaving the next day and it seemed impossible to consume all the milk and chocolate before our departure. Paul was perplexed; he had no explanation for his behavior.

At the next day's session Erickson asked, "What strange thing did Paul do when he left the session?" We were amazed! However, Erickson was not surprised at Paul's response, and in fact he interpreted it. In his induction he had been discussing polarities with Paul (e.g., red versus green vision). Paul could not achieve the effect even though he really wanted to, but he was primed to respond; since he had to do something, he went out and guided by his unconscious bought something black and something white!

Erickson recognized Paul's responsiveness and knew that his suggestions were going to have an effect, even if not the intended one.

*Summary*

The accuracy of Erickson's predictions certainly enhanced his credibility. Moreover, he took charge of the relationship and effectively disrupted habitual sets. Erickson was not just living off his reputation; he could deliver the goods.

## OBSERVING ERICKSON'S THERAPIES

I was able to sit in on a few sessions when Erickson did therapy with his patients. It was instructive to see firsthand some of his scope and range.

*Example One*

The following case is reported in another paper (Zeig, 1985a, p. 322). However, I recently found some of the notes that I made after the session and can add some new facts (Erickson, personal communication, 5/7/74).

I made my request to sit in on one of his sessions in the morning and Erickson denied it, explaining that it would probably be inappropriate for me to sit in with his private practice patients.

That afternoon, while he was seeing patients, I rested in the bedroom next door to Erickson's office. A knock aroused me from a nap. When I opened the door, a very attractive, conservatively dressed woman explained that Erickson wanted to see me.

I oriented myself and entered Erickson's office. The woman was seated in the patient's chair. Erickson said that he was not going to introduce me, I was just to sit down. He asked me what I saw. I replied, "A woman." The woman replied, "Three heads." She was playing with her sunglasses nervously and pursing her lips. Erickson picked up on the fact that she was shy, afraid, and wanted to leave. When she started to do so, he grasped her hand and asked her to stay.

Erickson said, "Kathy (fictitious name) has told me that she wears sunglasses to protect herself from the hostile world. But I told her that she didn't need those sunglasses in here with me." In fact, at the moment the sunglasses were on the end table near Kathy.

Suddenly, Erickson changed contexts and asked me, "Isn't she pretty?" I looked at Kathy and said, "Yes." Kathy asked if I were a psychology student and Erickson picked up on the fact that this was a discount. He said that I was a therapist from California.

Erickson continued by asking, "Doesn't she have beautiful features?" I looked at Kathy and said, "Yes."

"Doesn't she have beautiful eyes?" I looked at Kathy and said, "Yes," although I remember being a bit tentative in my response.

"Doesn't she have beautiful lips?" I looked at Kathy, gulped, and said, "Yes."

Erickson's next question was, "Aren't her lips kissable?" I started to sweat. Erickson became more animated, moving from side to side in his chair, speaking rapidly, one question following immediately after the next. "Doesn't she have lovely legs? Isn't she dressed well? Wouldn't she make a good wife? Don't you think that she is marriageable?"

Erickson bombarded her with compliments. He said that he knew that she would accept the compliments because of her pursed lips.

I was atwitter. I remember thinking, "Is she in a trance? Am I in a trance? Is she the patient? Am I the patient? What is the purpose? Is he trying to get me married?"

Erickson told her that he had two relatives named Kathy and that she was now his third Kathy. He wanted to establish a sense of belonging and decrease the possibility that she would see him as a threat.

He asked her to make a solemn promise to move to Phoenix, away from her domineering mother. The patient nodded that she would and promised to move after completing a business transaction. He had previously seeded the idea that she could have her business deal attended to by proxy. He said that he would take care of Kathy's domineering mother if Kathy moved to Phoenix, and that he would not let her influence the therapy.

Erickson continued to extract promises from her in a light vein. He said, "'When will you come to therapy?" She said, "The seventh." He said, "What month?" She replied, "June." He said, "What year?" She replied, "1974." Then he told her to put it all together. She said that she would do what he asked.

Erickson asked me if I felt that my cousin, Ellen, or his daughter, Kristi, could be friends with her. He pointed out things I had missed. She was single; she wasn't wearing an engagement ring.

The patient actually said little, but Erickson was quite active verbally and physically. When he was complimenting her, he bobbed back and forth in his wheelchair. He was not really in a therapeutic stance; he was personable and natural, protective towards her, and somewhat paternal. He was both caring and intense.

Suddenly Mrs. Erickson appeared and wheeled Erickson out of the office and I was left with Kathy. I said goodbye to Kathy and locked up Erickson's office. A few minutes later, there was a knock on the door and it was Kathy. In an embarrassed manner, she blurted out, "I forgot my sunglasses." Sure enough, her sunglasses were on the end table where she had left them.

After Kathy had left with her sunglasses, I went to the main house to tell Erickson about this "serendipitous" occurrence, thinking how much it would amuse him. But he indicated that he expected her response and in fact had set it up.

Kathy had come into his office wearing sunglasses and, when he suggested that she would not need the sunglasses with him, she put them on the table. Then he talked with her about other matters. During that discussion, he interspersed suggestions by casually looking at the sunglasses and explaining to Kathy, "You know how easy it is to leave something behind. For example, you have had times in which you forgot your purse." Then he went back to the previous topic of conversation. The result of Erickson's naturalistic technique was that Kathy forgot the sunglasses.

Erickson was obviously pleased with Kathy's response. He explained, "Her unconscious mind is starting to believe in me." He stated that he had used me in the session to reach Kathy because she had an almost delusional belief that there was something observably wrong with her. She had grown up in a family where disparaging remarks had been made about her sexuality and she went overboard in making her femininity known. Through his work, Erickson hoped that Kathy would learn to accept a compliment from a man in the presence of another man. Further she could live through this process with no ill effect. For my part, I learned something about my ability to endure pressure.

As far as I know, Kathy was not told that, in forgetting her sunglasses, she was responding to a naturalistic amnesia, to a suggestion that Erickson presented indirectly. I am also certain that Erickson did not interpret Kathy's responsive behavior back to her.

## Example Two

A young woman suffered from wildly fluctuating weight. When she was at college, she would gain weight, but when she was at home, she would lose it. (This case is reported in detail in Rosen, 1982a, p. 145.)

Erickson interpreted her behavior to me, explaining that she had to be a "little girl" at home. I asked if he would make that interpretation to the patient, and he definitely said, "No." He wanted her pattern to change, and he didn't think this interpretation would mobilize her.

In the session I observed, which was not reported in Rosen's account, he was working on an additional problem of test anxiety. He told a number of stories suggesting that she could do better when she was quiet, comfortable, and relaxed.

When she came out of the trance, Erickson indirectly indicated that she could let her unconscious mind close her eyes. When she hesitated, he interpreted her resistance as internal, not directed to him. He later told me that if she went along with his suggestion, she would have to agree that her body was okay, and that was something that she presently refused to do.

*Example Three*

After an induction, Erickson looked up at one woman who was rather negative. He caught her attention and said to her intensely, "When you look at a garden, you can either look at the flowers or you can look at the weeds." It was a memorable way of suggesting a positive perspective. That analogy had an enduring impact on me. I've used it effectively with numerous patients.

Having noted some of the methods Erickson favored for promoting change, I will present a transcript of my initial meeting with Erickson in December, 1973. Here the reader will be able to study Erickson in action and note not only the microdynamics of his methods but the process over time. As will be seen, commonsense advice will be presented, one-step removed through the dramatic description of cases and family vignettes.

CHAPTER 4

# Milton Erickson:
# A Transcript,
# December 3-5, 1973

To demonstrate powerful, multilevel therapeutic communication and Erickson's method of individually training a novice psychotherapist, my introduction to Erickson in December 3, 4, and 5, 1973 is presented. At the time I had just completed my Masters degree in clinical psychology and was working at a residential treatment center for severely disturbed patients. Before presenting the transcript and to set the stage, I will describe my initial meeting with Erickson from the beginning (Zeig, 1980a, pp. 19-20).

My initial introduction was quite unusual. At about ten-thirty at night, I arrived at Erickson's home. I was greeted at the door by Roxanna. She introduced me to her father, gesturing to Dr. Erickson, who was seated to the immediate left of the door watching television. She stated, "This is my father, Dr. Erickson." Erickson slowly, mechanically moved his head upward, in small stepwise movements.

When his head reached the horizontal level, he slowly, mechanically, using the same stepwise movements, twisted his head toward me. When he caught my visual attention and looked in my eyes, he again started the same mechanical, slow, stepwise movements and looked down the midline of my body. To say that I was quite shocked and surprised by this "Hello" would be an understatement. Nobody had ever said "Hello" to me like that before. For a moment I was cataleptic—frozen—and I didn't know what to do. Then Roxanna took me into the other room and explained that her father was a practical joker.

However, Erickson's behavior was not a practical joke. It was an excellent nonverbal hypnotic induction. All of the maneuvers necessary to induce hypnosis were presented in his nonverbal behavior toward me. He used confusion to disrupt my conscious set. I expected him to shake hands and say "Hello." Now I was lost for a response. I couldn't rely on customary patterns. Erickson was not merely using disruption; he was also patterning. He modeled the hypnotic phenomena he wanted me to experience—namely, the stepwise cataleptic movements that patients show, for example, when they do an arm levitation. His actions also focused my attention, which is one of the characteristics of trance. Then, when he looked down the midline of my body, he was suggesting to "go down inside," i.e., experience trance.

Erickson had provided me with an example of the power that he could put into communication.

DAY ONE, DECEMBER 3, 1973

The next morning, Erickson was wheeled into his guesthouse by Mrs. Erickson. Without saying a word or making any visual contact, he painfully transferred himself from his wheelchair to his office chair. I asked him if I could set up my tape recorder and without looking at me he nodded yes. Then he began to speak to the floor in a slow, measured way:*

---

* Editor's Note: Erickson's words are presented practically verbatim; only minor grammatical changes have been made to ensure readability. His speech was extraordinarily precise.

E: To aid you over the *shock* of all the purple. . . .

Z: Uh-huh.

E: I am partially color-blind.

Z: I realize that.

E: And the purple telephone . . . was a gift from four graduate students.

Z: Uh-huh.

E: Two of whom knew they would fail their majors . . . and two of whom knew they would fail . . . their minors. The two who knew they would fail their majors, but *pass* . . . their minors . . . passed all. The two who knew they would pass their majors and flunk their minors . . . flunked their majors and passed their minors. In other words, they selected the help I offered. (*E. looks at Z. for the first time and fixes his gaze.*)

This brief anecdote is an elegant piece of communication. It is actually a naturalistic confusion induction of hypnosis, containing many levels of message. One of the effects of the induction was my complete amnesia for it! (For a detailed description of Erickson's method and my responses see Zeig, 1980a.)

E: Concerning psychotherapy, most therapists overlook a basic consideration. Man is characterized not only by mobility but by cognition and by emotion, and man defends his intellect emotionally. And no two people necessarily have the same ideas, but all people will defend their ideas whether they are psychotically based or personally based. When you understand how man really defends his intellectual ideas and how emotional he gets about it, you should realize that the first thing in psychotherapy is not to try to compel him to change his ideation, rather you go along with it and change it in a gradual fashion and create situations wherein he himself willingly changes his thinking.

I think my first real experiment in psychotherapy occurred in 1930. A patient in Worcester State Hospital in Massachusetts demanded he be locked in his room, and he spent his time anxiously and fearfully winding string around the bars of the window of the room. He knew his enemies were going to come in and kill him, and the window was the only opening. The thin iron bars seemed to him to be too weak so he reinforced them with string.

I went into the room and helped him reinforce the iron bars with string. In doing so, I discovered that there were cracks in the floor and suggested that those cracks ought to be stuffed with newspaper so that there was no possibility (of his enemies getting him), and then I discovered cracks around the door that should be stuffed with newspaper. Gradually I got him to realize that the room was only one of a number of rooms on the ward, and to accept the attendants as a part of his defense against his enemies; and then the hospital itself as a part of his defense against his enemies; and then the Board of Mental Health of Massachusetts as part, and then the police system; and the governor. And then I spread it to adjoining states and finally I made the United States a part of his defense system, which enabled him to dispense with the locked door because he had so many other lines of defense.

I didn't try to correct his psychotic idea that his enemies would kill him. I merely pointed out that he had an endless number of defenders. The result was: the patient was able to accept ground privileges and wander around the grounds safely. He ceased his frantic endeavors. He worked in the hospital shops, and was much less of a problem. . . .

(Editor's Note: This second segment of the transcript is presented in Zeig, 1980b where it is discussed as an example of symptom prescription. The remainder of the transcript is previously unpublished.)

E: The next important learning I had was . . . to assume things about a patient is awfully wrong.

In the year 1900 or thereabouts, Jimmy was brought to the state hospital. If I recall correctly, his diagnosis was chronic idiocy. He was a schizophrenic, vegetating. He sat, he ate; he finally learned toilet habits. He came to the hospital when he was about 30 years old. He was given ground privileges and he wandered around the hospital grounds picking up twigs and leaves. I recall (*he was found with*) the mummified body of a toad that had been run over by a truck. Every evening the attendants emptied the trash out of his pockets. He seldom spoke. He showed no interest in anything. He ate, slept, filled his pockets with trash, and showed no resentments of his pockets being emptied of his treasures.

One day when I returned from Boston, there was a great deal of excitement. There had been a fire which involved the rooms on that ward. There were two attendants on that ward and about 40 patients. Both attendants had been frightened out of their wits by the fire. Jimmy arose to the occasion. He told one attendant, "Get all of the patients. Take them to a side door, then take them outside and count them. When you know that they're all there, take them over to that tree out in the yard and see to it they stay there."

To the other attendant he said, "Now, you give me your keys and come with me." And Jimmy searched every room, under the beds, and then locked each room after inspecting it carefully; he didn't miss a single possible hiding place. After the ward was fully inspected he took the frightened attendant out and gave him help in assisting the other attendant in watching the patients. Then he wandered off, picking up twigs and leaves and various other trash.

When I came back from Boston, the fire alarm had just quieted down. Not much damage was done. The patients were brought back to the ward and Jimmy came in, and sat in his usual corner of the ward, unchanged from the Jimmy I had known for several months. I asked him what had happened. He guessed something must have happened. He wasn't sure what had happened. I asked searching questions. I asked leading questions. But all he seemed to know was something must have happened. He really didn't know what. The two frightened attendants were very embarrassed in giving me an account of what did happen. Several patients who were much more in contact with reality confirmed their story about what Jimmy did. The two attendants were very much embarrassed that Jimmy, who had a diagnosis of chronic idiocy, 30 years an inmate at the hospital, had been much more competent than they had been.

So when you come to the mentally ill patient, you really don't know what you're dealing with.

It was purposeful that Erickson's first two anecdotes dealt with severely disturbed patients. One of the few facts Erickson knew about me was my interest in schizophrenia. In my initial letter I told him that I worked in a residential treatment center for chronic patients and sent a draft of an article I authored on auditory hallucinations (Zeig, 1974). Following his cardinal principle of meeting the patient at the patient's frame of reference, Erickson was speaking my experiential language, instructing me in my own area of interest and indirectly establishing commonalities.

Note that Erickson neither had much information about me, nor did he ask questions. He was much more verbally active than I. His style forced me to do a lot of processing. Erickson would tell his stories and learn about me from my responses. The direction he chose was dependent on my reactions. He did not need much input from me. Rather, he would generally determine his goals from his perception of my minimal, unconscious responses.

Erickson's primary goal was to instruct me in the art of psychotherapy. Simultaneously he would help me with my personal development. These goals were not stated in an explicit contract. However, they were clearly understood. The effect of all this ambiguity is that I was mildly (but comfortably) confused. Because I was not entrenched in a particular set, it would be easier to change.

There was another pattern to Erickson's communication. When he presented the case of the psychotic and the string, he was both presenting principles and providing illustration. For example, the case stated or alluded to the following ideas: 1) the necessity of not assuming things about patients; 2) the importance of gradual change; 3) meeting patients on their own ground; 4) creating situations for people to realize their *own* power to change their thinking.

In the next case (Jimmy), he embellished the point that clinicians should attend from the patient's perspective, not from preconceptions.

To effect the desired outcome, Erickson regularly used a three-step anecdotal method. One, when presenting a case, there would often be an introductory phrase that spoke in general terms to the concepts to be presented. Two, there would be an illustrative and dramatic case study(ies). (It was unusual that the first two anecdotes were case fragments. Especially in his later life, Erickson commonly told stories about successful therapy or about interesting life incidents. As a matter of practice, he did not tell about specific interventions unless they were successful.) Three, Erickson would present a summary statement elaborating on the ideas he had been emphasizing. This three-step pattern will be repeated throughout the transcript.

The lengths that Erickson would go to make his point would depend on my responses. It seemed that he would watch my minimal cues to see if I "got it" before he moved on to the next point. If I didn't, there would be further elaboration and additional cases for examples.

Note that there is purposeful vagueness in each step of the process, i.e., the concepts were often presented "one-step removed." I would have to work to get the point and it would be my efforts that energized the situation.

E: Now, in approaching the problem of psychotherapy you ought to try to learn what patients are saying to you, how they're saying it, and what they mean. Psychotherapy has been cursed with a lot of people with wonderful theoretical formulations. But so far, little has been done to promote psychotherapy in relationship to the patient in *his* situation of life. Instead, a theoretical body of concepts is formulated and then attempts are made to fit the patient to that Procrustean bed.

Now, do you know what I mean by a Procrustean bed?

Z: I have an idea.

E: It means the bed of Procrustes from Greek mythology. Travelers were offered a bed for the night. Those who were too long for the bed had the part that was protruding from the bed cut off. Those who were too short for the bed were stretched to fit it.

Now, I'm going to give you some typewritten material to read. It was taken down by my secretary. A charge nurse had been instructed by my office to tell me when a new patient entered the hospital who was talkative, noisy, and disturbed. My secretary had excellent stenographic ability. She could take down whatever the patient was saying, even as rapidly as court reporters do.

Of the three cases I'm going to give you, she recorded what two of them said. The other patient was one whose husband called me one morning when I was at the Induction Board in Detroit during World War II. The telephone call was to the effect that the Army had granted him a 60-day furlough to take his wife to a psychiatrist. The furlough would expire the next morning at 8 a.m., and his wish was that I see his wife at 6 p.m. that evening, because he had just gotten around to taking his wife to see a doctor.

Now, I wanted desperately to see that patient. I thought it should prove to be interesting so far as my thinking was concerned. So I met them in my office at 6 p.m. The woman made three remarks, and I stated, "Madam, I don't know anybody I hate enough to refer you to for medical assistance." That was in March.

The woman's reaction to that dismissal was to come out to the hospital the next visiting day. I had instructed my secretary to allow Diane (*all names are fictitious*) to sit down in the chair. I told her, "Do not speak to her, do not listen to her. She will talk. Make sure you do not speak to her." If I happened to be in the office at the time, I didn't speak. She came on visiting days. She would spend sometimes an hour or two hours in my office, talking to me about her children, Nicky and Joan. I never once replied. I listened. I knew that Joan was a girl's name. I knew that Nicky could be a boy's name or a girl's name. She used the pronouns "she" and "her" for Joan. So far as Nicky was concerned, she just said, "Nicky." She said, "Nicky's playthings, Nicky did this, Nicky did that. Nicky ate breakfast. Nicky learned something new. Nicky went to the park with her."

One day I received a phone call from the charge nurse who said that we had a new patient named Diane, who was talking volubly, and she stated, "Diane is undergoing the admission procedure."

I went to a very brilliant resident in psychiatry and told him I had a new patient on the ward. I was going to assign her to him because I knew she would be most educational to him. I had some instructions. He was to take half a dozen or a dozen sharpened pencils and give them and plenty of blank paper to an attendant. He was to station Diane at a table, explain that he was going to be her therapist, and that he wanted her to write her life history for him. He was also to station an attendant beside that table who was to seize each page when Diane completed filling that page, keep it, and not let Diane make any corrections, changes, alterations, erasures, or anything.

Diane wrote enough to fill 37 pages of double-spaced type-writing on a very hot, sultry, muggy day, in the late afternoon. And Diane wrote feverishly. Her written material was brought down to my secretary, who had been instructed to type it up carefully and then lock it up in a special drawer to which she had the only key. "I don't want to know what's in it, and I don't want anybody else to know."

The resident was delighted when he saw the patient the next day. He stated she was a most charming patient, eager and willing for psychotherapy, and that he seemed to be making excellent progress. He saw her on Monday. Saturday he was almost in tears because he had made some kind of stupid mistake and caused the patient to regress back to the point at which she entered.

I told him that mistakes are always made by everybody, not to be concerned, but to continue and see if he could correct his error. For the next two weeks, the resident walked on air, Diane was so responsive. He even gave up his Sunday in order to work with Diane. After two weeks, he was again reduced to the verge of tears. He had again made some stupid mistake and set Diane back to her state when she first entered the hospital. For three months, he made mistake after mistake. Diane always recovered the ground that she lost and made further progress.

At the end of three months, he made another bad mistake and set her back to her original condition. He came to me and said, "I know I can make mistakes, but nobody can make as many mistakes as I've made with Diane. Nobody could make that number of mistakes, and it seems I have. Would you please tell me what's been going on? I think I've been played as a yo-yo." So then I took him to my office and told my secretary, "Bring out the life story that Diane wrote out." I gave it to him and told him to read it and tell me whatever he could about Diane. I related to him that she had made three remarks to me on that day in March, to which I replied, "I don't know anybody I hate enough to refer you to for psychiatric help." And I also related how Diane had come every visiting day to talk, either to my secretary or to me, often talking about Nicky and Joan.

E. *(to Zeig):* I'll give you that case record.*

If you will read the first paragraph, you will know everything about Diane. If you read the second paragraph, you will know not only everything, but you will have proof. If you read the third paragraph, you'll have not only complete knowledge of Diane and proof, but her method. And the fourth paragraph will confirm everything.

My question to you is, "What did she write on the last page?"—Don't look. Do your own thinking because if you read the first four paragraphs, you should know exactly what's on the last page of the manuscript. (Erickson gives Zeig two more case records.)

Now then, here are—I call them stenograms, because my secretary used a stenotype machine—of Eva Parton.** All you need to read, of course, is the first paragraph for a diagnosis; the first page for her occupation; and the last page to know her age. Upon completion of the second page, you'll have all the proof in the world that you need to confirm her diagnosis, her age, her occupation, and to realize the significant events of her life.

The third stenogram is on Millie Parton† (*no relationship to Eva Parton*). You read the first page and the second page and you should know everything that Millie has told you. You should

---

* See Appendix A for the first and last pages of the biography written by this patient. The entire 37 pages are on file in the Erickson Foundation Archives.
** See Appendix B for the entire four page transcript.
† See Appendix C for the first four pages. The entire ten-page transcript is on file in the Erickson Foundation Archives.

know it very completely. You can read all of the other pages, if you want to, and you'll know *everything* that she's told you. Of course, you'll know her diagnosis. You'll also be able to prove to yourself that you can read and understand what you're reading.*

I have a patient coming in at 12 o'clock. You can busy yourself for the hour that she is here by reading this material. While I see the patient, you can go over the first two pages on Eva Parton, as much as you care to read of Millie Parton, and the first page of Diane. Then at one o'clock, I'll quiz you to see if you even read the material. Because most people don't know how to read. They don't know how to listen. There's a tendency in people to hear what they want to hear, to think what they want to think, to understand as they want to understand. Not to understand what the patient is saying or writing. They try to put what they hear or read in the framework of their own experience, and that isn't the way to do psychotherapy. You listen to the *patient*. You understand the *patient*.

Now, to interrupt, I don't know exactly what you want to get out of seeing me, but I have no intention of letting you leave here without having acquired some understanding of what human communication is, how human beings think and react and how they behave, and how they think they're thinking about themselves and about the world around them.

These are three informative cases. I had my residents in psychiatry read these transcripts until finally they could go into a locked room where a disturbed, noisy patient was confined, and listen and come down and state the diagnosis correctly. Of course, they didn't always do it. Sometimes it took several months for them to realize what they had heard and what they should have understood immediately. But it was a delightful teaching experience, and a delightful learning experience.

Now, when I'm out of the office, if you wish to look around in here, you're entirely welcome. I won't give you too much time for the reason that physically I'm not able to do so. I see one or

---

* Editor's note: In order to benefit most from the following discussion, the reader should study the transcripts and try to answer Erickson's questions before reading much further.

two patients a day, particularly interesting patients—patients I think that I can help with a minimum of effort. I have one patient coming in today and two tomorrow.

The patient coming in today has already told me, without knowing it, that she doesn't yet want to get over her problem, and she doesn't want to know that she wants to get over it, nor does she want to know that she doesn't want to get over it. She has indicated to me that there shall be a definite period of time (*before getting over it*) but what that period of time shall be, she hasn't let me know. I know some of her reasons for not getting over her problem, but she has described them mistakenly. I had Dr. Ernest Rossi watch the patient and let him see her indicate that she didn't want to get over the problem now. She knew her problem and knew that she would get over it, but she did not know the time of her recovery. And that she did not want to know it was emphatically manifested.

I think I have two new patients coming in tomorrow. If a patient comes in that I can let you see, I will do so. But most psychiatric patients don't want to disclose their problems to strangers.

E: All right, now what general questions do you have?

Z: Oh, on that case you were just talking about—the woman that you will be seeing, what was the ailment—what was the problem she was experiencing?

E: She said she had a phobia for flying planes.

Z: What were the indicators that she was not going to give up her phobia?

E: Do you have a pencil?

Z: I have a pen.

*(Erickson draws three lines on a sheet of paper. One horizontal, one vertical, and one diagonal.)*

E: Can you read that? *(pause)* Now the "yes" is characterized by a vertical line.

Z: Uh-huh.

E: The "no" is characterized by a horizontal line.

Z: Uh-huh.

E: Patients do not need to know that they are in a hypnotic trance.
   It's perfectly all right to let them think that they are not. Why
   should you argue the point with them? If you know that they're
   in a trance, that's sufficient.

At the time I had doubts about my ability to achieve trance. Perhaps
Erickson recognized this and was indirectly addressing my positive
response to the naturalistic confusion induction he previously presented.

E: When you lecture to an audience on a controversial subject, you
   watch the audience while you lecture. You'll see people doing
   this *(nodding)*. You'll also see them doing this *(shaking their head)*.
   At the end of the lecture you have a question and answer period.
   You point to one of these *(head nodder)*. Ask him what he thinks
   about what you've stated, and he warmly supports your views.
   Then you ask another *(head nodder)* and a third and a fourth.
   Then you pick out one who moves his head this way *(shakes his
   head)* and he will hesitatingly present his views. And then you
   ask another one *(head nodder)* and then you ask another *(head
   shaker)*. He even more weakly expresses his doubts. And nobody
   in the audience knows what you did. Because the audience wasn't
   watching the lecture.

Z: Knows what you did?

E: Yes, they heard the lecture. They think that everybody agrees with
   you. Nobody seemed to disagree.
      Now, "I don't know" is not "Yes." It's not "no." It's this
   *(Erickson diagonally tilts his head and laughs)*. And when they tilt
   their head and move it that way, they don't know. So you can
   pick the head nodders and shakers, and you know which ones
   to call on.

Erickson presented his information about minimal cues dramatically
and illustrated with powerful anecdotes. As a result, these simple
ideas came alive and became indelibly imprinted on my mind.

E: And in inducing trances in a group, you use your eyes—you see what's going on. Because very few people ever realize that they keep nodding.

Z: Excellent.

E: *(laughs)*. And so from this woman, while she was talking about her phobia, she was talking about her phobia in this way *(shakes his head no)*. And this way *(puts his head in the "I don't know" position)*. I could see that she used minimal movements to tell me that she was being careful because large movements could be recognized by the self, but minimal movements could be made without awareness.

And so you ask your questions cautiously and you wait for minimal movements. You see minimal movements when the patient is being cautious not to betray to the self; they are communicating with you but not with themselves, because the unconscious mind works in its own way.

Consciously we think, and we know where we are—the time of day, the time of the week, month and year—but we really don't know what goes on in the unconscious mind.

You've had plenty of experience meeting people and for presumably no reason at all disliking them. It may take you months to find out why you dislike them for the simple reason that we learn in our culture not to disclose certain things. We learn that we should never show certain behaviors. That tendency to repress and keep things in the unconscious marks human behavior. This is an advantage because the conscious mind should be *oriented* to the present situation.

Now you can listen to me without bothering to notice when the heater goes on or off; you don't need to recognize that stimulus. You don't need to notice consciously the bookcases in the room, the filing cases in the room, the purple colors in this room. But consciously you cannot free your conscious awareness of the tape recorder, the desk, the envelope, the cushion, my position. You have multiple foci of attention. In hypnosis you simply reduce the number of foci of attention, until your subject may have only one focus for the attention. And that focus may be stated very simply, because in hypnosis the patient can hear you with their eyes open, they don't need to see you to hear you, nor to consciously hear you to understand you. So you limit their foci of attention to the sound of your voice and the meaning of your words.

In addition to discussing the nature of hypnosis, this last section was another naturalistic induction. Note how Erickson guided my attention and used ambiguous pronouns to present suggestions, e.g., "In hypnosis *you (my italics)* simply reduce the number of foci of attention."

> *(Telephone rings and Erickson answers it. The call was from his son, Robert Erickson)*

E: Now, this matter of observation: Part of our training is to see things, and part of our training in our culture is to not see things. You overlook mispronunciations of someone speaking to you; you'd rather not see the egg on somebody's tie; you don't want to call a man's attention to his open fly when he's addressing an audience. You ignore so many things.

Now, I've trained myself to see an awful lot about patients and people. I usually turn off my gaze when I meet people socially, because what I could see about them is none of my business. When they come to me as patients, the more I can see about them, the better, because patients will tell you terrible lies.

I gave this woman I don't know how many opportunities to tell me that she had in her handbag a bottle containing whiskey—that she was an alcoholic, although she kept that secret.

(Telephone rings. Erickson talks with a therapist in Detroit, agreeing to see a patient that the therapist referred.)

E: Now that woman withheld that information from me, and I finally had to resort to asking her to let me see her driver's license, because I thought that part of her anxiety had to be the fact that her driver's license was about to expire. When she showed me the driver's license, I pointed out she had a week in which to take the test, and was she going to take it, and what was holding her back. And only then did she disclose her alcoholism. But she had told me a hell of a lot of things she didn't believe she would ever tell anybody about herself. One of them I surprised out of her by noting a self-revealing nonverbal communication which she, herself, didn't understand.

This story about the phobic woman certainly directed my thinking. I wondered what I was communicating nonverbally and I thought about my own "hidden" difficulties.

E: Now, nonverbal communication: During World War II, I was working at the Induction Board, and I rode a bus from Detroit to Wayne County General Hospital. One afternoon, when I was returning to Wayne County General Hospital, I was at a window seat on the bus. A young man got on and sat down beside me. He didn't speak and I didn't speak. The bus rode along over Livernois Avenue and came to the area where Henry Ford had his apple orchard.

Curiously, I watched the young man's eyeballs. I saw his eyeballs measure the length of the orchard—the width of the orchard, and then the number of bushel baskets of apples that the pickers would place at the end of the orchard near the highway. The young man murmured to himself, "Fair to Medium." It was an assessment of the crop. There was no indication of anything else.

I asked, "Where was the farm you grew up on?" Only a farmboy with some knowledge of crops could ask that question. And he said, "Virginia." And then he had unconsciously noted that I had asked him a farmboy question. He said, "Where was the farm you grew up on?" I said, "Wisconsin," and the conversation ended. It never occurred to him to ask me how I knew to ask him that question.

(At this point Erickson takes a break in the session. He gives Zeig the three transcripts and sees his 12 o'clock patient. The session resumes:)

E: How much of the Eva Parton case have you read?

Z: I read the whole thing on Eva.

E: All right, how much of Millie Parton?

Z: I read about 5 or 6 pages. And then I read just the first two pages of Diane.

E: All right. First, what do you think about Eva Parton? (*See Appendix B*)

Z: OK. She seems like she was really protecting herself. She says she offers the opportunity to ask questions, but she doesn't really allow questions to be asked. So what I get from that is that she's really protecting some aspects of herself. One of the things I was thinking is that she might be afraid of. . . .

E: (*overlapping*) What has she told you?

Z: What has she told me? OK.

E: Uh-huh.

Z: What I understand about her is that she doesn't have a very good understanding of where she stands as a person. (*to Erickson*) You're not asking for an analytical description. It's difficult for me because I was looking for analytical descriptions.

E: I can summarize. She said nothing at all.

Z: (*laughs*)

E: Absolutely nothing. And you didn't pick it up. You were analyzing nothingness.

Z: (*laughs*)

E: "You just ask questions, and I'll answer them." That's two positive statements. "Don't tell me you don't know that." That's two negatives.

Z: Yes.

E: "I'm 32 years old, or I'm supposed to be 32 years old."

Z: Uh-huh.

E: "Supposed to be" contradicts—"I am 32 years old."
   "I was born July 6, 1912 in Meridian, Missouri (*fictitious name*). It's a small town—gossip, over the back fence like dishwater—like dishwater slop that you throw out to the pigs."
   That doesn't tell a thing about the town, does it?

Z: No.

E: You don't even know it's a town. (*laughs*)

"Two-legged sluts and snakes in the form of human beings."

Snakes are not in the form of human beings. Do you know any snakes in the form of human beings? She hasn't told you anything. And two-legged sluts. What does that mean? She hasn't told you which two-legged sluts—who they are.

Z: I thought perhaps that was her conception of men and women.

E: "There are a lot of people that I don't like." Now you could call that statement a positive and a negative.

"One of them is the lady that raised me."

No lady raises—a lady rears. So she ain't no lady. (*Erickson laughs*)

Z: Uh-huh.

E: "I worshipped the man who raised me. He was as white as a lily, and his hair was as black as a raven."

So she mentions black against white. Contradicting white with "black as a raven."

Z: Uh-huh.

E: She's just speaking about color, though. You thought she was saying something about someone.

Z: Uh-huh.

E: "His eyes were yellow as leopards, but he was one leopard that never changed his spots."

If she worshipped the man, the most she told you about him was that he had yellow eyes. Black contradicts white, and leopards don't change their spots. (*Erickson laughs*) "He was light, her mother was dark." White-dark—contradictory again.

"He had an older brother who dominated the family and he put his wife in the insane asylum." When you put your wife in an insane asylum, you don't have a wife.

"She's in another place now." Contradicting the preceding statement.

Z: Uh-huh.

E: "When they have padded cells so you don't dash your brains out." Another contradiction. Now she was put in another insane asylum.

"She was released under his care, 18 years ago, and the dirty lousy son-of-a-bitch got her pregnant." Then she was put back—contradictory.

And "Her *little* boy is now 18 years old." What little boy is 18 years old? No 18-year-old is a little boy.

"My sister-in-law Norma Kowalski, the wife of my half-brother, Jacob Kowalski, who lives at 12345 Braile in Detroit. . . ." That sounds like a street number, doesn't it?

Z: Yes.

E: But you can say 1-2-3-4-5 faster than you can give a street number. 3-4-2-8-5, for example. She gave a series of numbers that she could utter most rapidly.

Z: I see.

E: *(reading the end of the transcript)* "In the Bible it tells you a whore is someone who sells her body, but I never sold my body, but I intend to when I get out of this place because I'm tired of working so damned hard for what I get out of this world, and I'm not going to work anymore."

Contradictions, one after another. You're left with a wealth of nothingness.

Z: There are lots of different things in there to pick up and interpret and analyze.

E: It has nothing to do with. . . .

Z: *(overlapping)* really looking at the balance she creates.

E: Looking at the balance she creates.

Z: And it adds up to nothing.

E: And it adds up to nothing. And the folly of trying to analyze that—interpret it.

Z: Uh-huh.

E: When she recovered from her manic phase, she wrote me a letter—all recovered. That time she gave me information about herself.

"Yesterday I did bake a cake, but I'm not baking a cake today."

Z: The same thing.

E: The same balance, but with actual statements. Nothing that really redeemed her as a person. You're right in saying that she was protecting herself. But protecting herself by making noises.

Z: And would the issue in doing therapy with somebody like that be to respect their desire not wanting to reveal anything about themselves. How would you approach working with her?

E: Let her talk away: "Yell away, make all the noise you want to. Sooner or later, you'll listen to me. And then I may be able to listen to you."

Z: Meeting her resistance and providing a lot of caring. "I'm available to you when you're ready."

E: Telling her, "I'm going to listen to you and you make all the noise you want to. *(softens his voice)* And maybe sometime you will listen to me." That gives her the opportunity of disputing that or accepting it.

Z: All this noise is so that she doesn't have to listen to you.

E: Uh-huh. And telling her that she doesn't control my behavior. I'm free to do what I please, and maybe she will listen to me. She can't dispute that statement without admitting its meaning, and she can't agree without admitting its meaning—either way, I've got her.

I used that idea in one of my techniques. The American Psychiatric Association thought about expelling me. I gave a paper on the desirability of physical restraint. They cancelled other concurrent meetings to listen to my paper. Friends warned me not to read the paper. I went ahead. I pointed out that psychiatric patients often squeeze in between the mattress and the springs of a bed and hide in dark corners. They retire into dark corners and hide, wrap themselves up in an effort to protect themselves. I found out that I could put patients into straitjackets and thereby meet the needs of hiding. I'd tell the patient, "As soon as you feel comfortable, all you have to do is ask the nurse to take it off."

Z: Then you were saying, "I'm not going to be straitjacketed by your attempts."

E: Yes. I had my patients put in straitjackets. It might take 15 minutes to put the patient in. By the time the straitjacket was laced up the patient would say, "I think you can take me out, now." And the nurse would have to undo it. The nurses hated it, but my patients liked it. And they knew they could call for a straitjacket any time. I thought it was far better than hiding between the mattress and the springs or behind the door.

At the same time Eva was getting better, Mrs. Erickson and

I had been pondering this question of puns on names. What kind of a pun can you make of the name, Erickson? We couldn't think of any. The next morning, when I was on the ward, Eva said to me, "Can I have a cigarette, Dr. Erickson?" I said, "No, Eva." She said, "That's all right, Dr. Irksome." Absolutely beautiful. *(Erickson laughs)*

Z: Uh-huh.

E: Now that's one bit of material that you've read without knowing what you were reading. What about Millie Parton . . . diagnosis, her age, her occupation? *(See Appendix C)*

Z: Um. I dislike labels. I'd say a diagnosis of being schizophrenic and paranoid. Age, I have no idea. Occupation, I don't know.

E: All right. Regardless of your dislike of labels, "First of all, I'm not a patient here." Where was she?

Z: *(laughs)*

E: What kind of unreality was she expressing?

Z: Uh-huh.

E: "I was brought here by my aunt two days ago. I'm quite certain my aunt had good intentions." No paranoid ever credited anybody else with good intentions. So here's unreality that permits good intentions.

"She thought I needed some treatment of some sort. Just what, I haven't the vaguest notion." Now what kind of mental disorder do you have when you haven't got the vaguest notion of anything? *(Erickson laughs)*

"They had me in Bellevue in New York City while I was there. I have been living there off and on for the past three years. I might say mostly off, because my husband has been in the service all that time. . . ."

Now what kind of a patient can, with a straight face, say, "I'd been living there off and on. I might say mostly off. . . ." She was really off base. The type of patient called catatonic praecox. Nobody would agree with me until some months later she developed a catatonic stupor.

"Off and on." There's a sly bit of humor—"mostly off." Sly humor that isn't recognizable for what it is. Only the catatonic praecox can give that sly humor, because they're standing off from themselves and looking on with amusement.

Z: Uh-huh.

E: "My uncle raised me and he was very good to me. I was happy
    there until I grew up. Then—well, I think everyone gets to an
    age where they want to have their own home. There's nothing
    wrong or unnatural about that, is there?"

    At what age do you have to be to give that middle-aged phi-
    losophy?

Z: Say, about 40ish?

E: That's right. You have to be. It's a middle-aged expression, a
    middle-aged philosophy. *(to Zeig)* Now, can you confirm that?

    "Why there should be anything wrong with using a German
    name, I don't know. But it seems that every time there's a war
    in this country, people with German names have one hell of a
    time."

    So she was around during World War I.

Z: I see.

E: *(laughs)* Now, on this page, there's absolute proof of her occupation.

Z: There is?

E: Uh-huh. And it spells three letters.

Z: Three letters?

E: It's named with several words and then proved by a three-letter
    word.

*(Long pause as Zeig studies the material)*

Z: OK. I give up.

E: She's a woman of the world.

Z: A woman of the world? You mean a prostitute?

E: Yes. *(laughs)* "And Chris has been out in the world, *too*."

    So things got bad at the Henry Hudson Hotel, so she moved
    to another hotel. And then she moves back to another hotel.

Z: Uh-huh.

E: She worked the hotels. *(to Zeig)* Why don't you understand what
    you read?

    What do you know about Diane? *(see Appendix A)*

Z: One of the things that I was thinking was that you made an in-
    tervention that was potent. It seemed that she was looking to see
    if she could find somebody that was really strong—somebody
    that she couldn't manipulate; that she couldn't control. Also,

her anger, her being really angry, in a sort of indirect way, is really apparent.

E: Now what do you know about her?

Z: I'm doing it again, huh? *(laughs)*

E: *(pause)* Remember she made three remarks to me—I told her I didn't know anybody I hated enough to refer her to.

Z: What were the three remarks?

E: Well, you ought to be able to figure them out. You ought also to know what's on the last page. In the first paragraph, four people are mentioned derogatively.

Z: Uh-huh.

E: In the next paragraph, what is mentioned?

Z: Stealing.

E: And a piano bench—mentioned derogatively.

Z: Uh-huh.

E: A diamond lavalier is classed with dime banks. You don't class diamonds with dime banks; they're not in the same category. Also, she mentions a fifth person derogatively.

   *(paraphrasing the third paragraph)* We had so much coal, we couldn't get it into the basement. People used to stand and curse. The only warmth that she can get is when she shows "the proper amount of gratitude."

   *(from the fourth paragraph)* And her earliest memory of her pretty mother was what?

Z: Reaching out and touching her dress.

E: Her dress—not her mother.

Z: It's a memory of a dress. That was the earliest memory of her mother—touching her dress.

E: All right. She came into my office and said, "I have a terrible headache. And that mess on your secretary's desk made my headache worse. And you would think a doctor could have more decent furniture. Anyone who reads medical books ought to know how to line them up properly on a shelf."

Z: Everything derogatory.

E: Everything derogatory. And poor Alex doing psychotherapy on her—she played him like a yo-yo. One week up, and down the next, until he knew he couldn't make all those mistakes.

Z: Uh-huh.

E: Then Danny became her doctor at his own request. He said, "I know what's wrong with you guys—why didn't you do a GI examination on Diane?" I said, "Probably because we're too stupid." Danny told us, "Well, I've ordered a complete GI series of her." I asked, "What time does she go to get her plates?"

We found out what time she would return after the first X ray, so Alex and I stood next to the elevator when Diane returned. She got off the elevator and said, "I've got a decent doctor, now." I said, "That's fine, Diane." She stepped around the corner; I hesitated a moment, and then we stepped around the corner. Diane was at the drinking fountain, swallowing all the water she could in order to ruin the second X ray. When she saw us, she said, "Damn you, smart aleck." She went into the women's room, and Alex and I weren't gentlemen—we also walked in. And there was Diane, with her finger down her throat, trying to vomit up the barium.

Well, she succeeded in ruining that series. So Danny sent her over for a second series. He got the first plate and she escaped from the hospital; came back two days later. He ordered a third X ray series. She escaped for the second time; came back a few days later. He ordered a fourth series. This time he put her in complete restraint and got a complete series of X ray plates. So she escaped from the hospital and didn't return for three months. (*Erickson laughs*) In other words, she was a sociopath who would destroy anything and everybody.

Z: What's on the last page?

E: Can't you guess?

Z: No.

E: I told Alex to station an attendant beside the table and give Diane a dozen pencils, and have the attendant seize each sheet after she had finished writing.

Z: Right.

E: I told him about how she came from March to August on visiting days and talked to the secretary or me, neither of whom gave any evidence of listening to her. She would talk about Joan, she's such a sweet girl; and Nicky likes to play games. Nicky likes pancakes. But never a pronoun in connection with Nicky's name. Now, you try to talk about two people and betray the sex of one easily, but don't betray the sex of the other.

Early in August, I had an errand on the hospital grounds. I came around the corner, and I saw Diane with Nicky and Joan. And I said, "I apologize, Diane. It was completely unintentional on my part to see you like this."

And she said, "God Damn your soul." Because then, I knew Nicky's sex. She then got even with me by going downtown to Detroit and getting a Detroit judge to commit her to Wayne County Hospital. And she was a resident of Pontiac County, and didn't belong in a Wayne County institution. *(Erickson laughs)* She made the judge make a mistake.

Z: So she would have to be under your care.

E: Under my care. She knew when the attendant stood there that I was responsible for her writing her life story, even if Alex did tell her he was to be her psychotherapist.

On the last page it says: "You suggested the hospital. I didn't want to—yet I knew I would. I thought back—the receiving ward—snotty attendants—afraid to leave—tired—ashamed to complain of physical ailments that worried me—because even when I had appendicitis in the hospital, they laughed and told me it was 'all in my head'—everything in Pontiac is 'all in your head.'

"You know the rest. I wish I had the courage to die first, and then I could see your face and bawl myself out. I thought you must believe I could get well, or you wouldn't give me your time. . . ."

*(to Zeig)* I didn't give her any of my time. *(Erickson laughs and continues reading)*

"I'm afraid I'll fail you. I'm not very brave. I know that. Underneath, my mind isn't a nice thing at all. I'll probably do anything to keep you from knowing it.

"That's all. I've written this *fast*, just as it came to me. It isn't a masterpiece, and the writing is poor." *(Erickson laughs)*

*(to Zeig)* She's comprehensive in derogating things—even the story of her life and the handwriting. *(Continues reading)*

"However, it gave me a sore arm, a stiff neck, and my head is very tired.

"I can't finish the story of my life as I'm not dead yet. I'm not even sure I want to die anymore—but—oh, how I hate to get up in the morning!"

She put a quotation from a song to end her life story. *(Erickson laughs)* In a mental hospital—"Oh, how I hate to get up in the morning!" She derogates the entire thing—the handwriting, the paper, herself, the story itself, and fills the entire thing with lies.

I came around the corner and saw the two kids—I found two little girls. I apologized to Diane—"I didn't intend to meet you this way." "God damn your soul" she said. *(Erickson laughs)*

Z: And her purpose was?. . . .

E: To force me to ask Nicky's sex. But I wondered how long Diane could keep it up.

Z: Obviously very artful.

E: Diane escaped from the hospital for the final time. Danny was angered because she fled to Albuquerque. One morning the mail was being distributed at the hospital. Danny's secretary told me, "Danny has heard from Diane." So I called Alex and we both went down to Danny's office to wait for him to pick up his mail. He picked it up and looked at it. He said, "Diane writes to me, not to you two!" And Danny opened the letter and started reading it, and his face reflected pleasure. Diane had written a beautiful, poetic prose description of the mountain scenery. But, the second paragraph began, "Tomorrow I'm going fishing at the bass hole."

*(Erickson to Zeig)* "Bass hole—asshole." *(Erickson laughs)*

E: *(continuing)* Danny read that line and said, "God damn her!" and threw the letter on the floor. That beautiful prose *(Erickson laughs)* followed by that vulgarity.

Fifteen years later she called me up. She said, "I'm in Phoenix now. I'm going to see a *good* doctor. I still got those headaches. I'm going to see Dr. St. George." So I called up Dr. St. George and said, "John, you have a new patient, Diane Chow of Albuquerque, New Mexico. She's a former patient of mine when I was in Michigan. Do you want to learn about her the easy way from me? Or do you want to learn about her the hard way?" He said, "The hard way sounds more interesting." So he started her on a series of skull X rays and angiograms. When he was halfway through the tests Diane left the hospital without authorization. She went to New Mexico and left St. George to pay her hospital bill. He called up and said, "I learned the hard way."

Here's a letter Diane wrote to me in 1967.* *(Erickson reads)* "Dr. Erickson, don't pretend you've forgotten me. I know you haven't.

"I'll make no excuses for my large writing, except to explain that my sight is poor, and that I must write through a magnifying glass (and, if you can't read it, you're blinder than I am). *(Erickson laughs)* Surprisingly, this opened up a whole new vista to me. I could no longer read much, nor paint, and it was amazing how useful ones eyes are. But I discovered two talents, one for bumping into everything, and, the other one, music. I play the organ, and there isn't much I can't play by ear within minutes." *(to Zeig)* In other words, she can teach herself by listening to the song once and then she plays it immediately. But not from the printed music. She just trusts her memory. You can't trust your memory for new songs. In other words, she's a haphazard player and contents herself. *(continues reading the letter)* "I met a colleague of yours (he claimed to be a friend but he didn't know how well I knew you). *(Erickson laughs)*

"In the first place, I doubt you'd want to call many men 'friend' and in the second place, I know your opinion of the ability of most psychiatrists, and, in the third place, he was a rosy cheeked ass, no less."

*(to Zeig)* From 1944 to 1967.

Z: Twenty-three years—no change.

E: That's right. All you had to listen to were those three statements— "Your secretary's desk was a mess, your furniture was cheap, all those medical books, and you don't appreciate them enough to put them in line."

And you don't analyze that. You just hear it, and understand

---

* This entire letter is on file at the Erickson Archives in Phoenix.

it. And know that any information you get from her is completely unreliable.

Poor Alex—three months and many of his weekends sacrificed to learn. Because you don't believe everything you hear, and you don't analyze everything you hear. You just understand what it means.

Z: Then it was clear that there was no intervention—there was nothing that could be done.

E: That's right. You could lose plenty.

Z: But there's nothing to be gained.

E: Nothing for her to gain, and nothing for you to gain. But I saw to it that Alex got some experience. *(Erickson laughs)* And Diane was furious at me for using her to give Alex experience.

Z: And she is still. . . .

E: *(overlapping)* unchanged. And St. George learned the hard way. It was his choice. He called and told me about it— "I learned the hard way." I said, "Would you have believed me if I had told you that she would make you a loser, no matter what you did?" He said, "No, I wouldn't have. She was charming, like-able. She's attractive, but she really knows how to play you for a sucker."

Z: I always feel that even with people who are really difficult that there must be some way of making an intervention, if I just had enough skill or enough experience, then—

E: You'd better get rid of that idea fast. Because what you're saying is—there must be some way to prevent death. There must be some way to prevent all diseases—if you had enough skill.

Z: Not so much a way to prevent. At least a way to cure or deal with it.

E: I think you have to recognize that you can't cure all diseases, but that's what a lot of stupid psychotherapists think. They've got the grandiose idea that they could cure everyone if they had enough skill—and that surely they could find that skill within them—instead of facing the fact that there are plenty of people that are not treatable, who will misuse treatment.

Discussing the case of Diane with Erickson affected me in a number of ways: 1) It helped me to understand that no matter how skilled the practitioner, therapy has definite limitations. I came to Erickson because he was so successful. Yet the first detailed case that he discussed with me was one in which he had no success and in which he didn't even attempt psychotherapy. It is important to work within the realm of what is practical and possible. Erickson wouldn't take just anyone as a patient; he wouldn't work with every type of problem. He knew where to apply his energy. 2) I could now recognize, understand, and address Diane's type of pattern. I would know how to deal with that particular kind of patient in the future. 3) I could look for predictable patterns in clinical work with all types of patients, especially those patterns that showed up in language usage. 4) Gradually I began to realize that Erickson's method was based on the level of the patient's response to the therapist's communication. If there is no responsiveness—no learning—there is no therapy, no matter how creative the therapist's technique. 5) I had a reaction on a personal level. I remember thinking to myself, "I am going to change."

Erickson continued by providing an example of a similar pattern. I guess he wanted to be sure that I "got it."

E: Now a general practitioner in Phoenix sent me a patient who suffered from pain in his thigh. He had been treating that patient by giving him drugs. The patient came in and described the pain to me. I recognized it was a good description—as good as I could find in any medical textbook. The patient expressed his distress because he was causing the doctor so much trouble. He told me that he was an engineer. He knew where he could retrieve a lot of expensive machinery lost in accidents of some sort. It was a very reasonable story. Of course, he would need $100 or so in order to start to finance the job. I asked him how much he'd hooked the general practitioner for. He said that he had borrowed $500, which had been insufficient, so he had borrowed another $500. He thought if he could borrow $100 from me, he'd be sure to be able to retrieve the equipment and make all three of us rich.

I said, "Do you really think I'm that stupid? You found a good way to get free drugs on a regular basis. And from a source the narcotics squad won't question. It's very evident that you read about the pain and recognized how easily you could get drugs. You've been swindling the family physician out of money, and you would like to add me to your list of suckers. I'm going to tell your family doctor."

The family doctor was irate with me for not being sympathetic to that patient. Many years later he and his wife and daughter came to me. He said, "I know that I mortgaged everything. I know I promised my wife I wouldn't put a mortgage on the house because she owned it. But I mortgaged the house and I still got to give that man more money because I know he can get back what I've invested in him."

His wife said, "We've lost our home; lost property we had; lost my jewelry, and the wedding presents. We had to take our kids out of college, and the damned fool wants to lend that crook some more money."

I told him, "If a patient gives you a textbook picture of a painful disease—expresses reluctance about narcotics, and asks for reassurance that he will not become addicted—you had better know immediately that he's a drug addict. And if you loan $500 to a man, you don't loan him $500 more to help him pay back the first $500.

He loaned more than $30,000 from his savings account before he lost his wife's home, and deprived his kids of a college education. They were out on their own, working for themselves, and he was really haggard from overwork. He got so greedy for money (he needed it to loan to the swindler) that he lost a lot of patients.

Why does a patient come to you? I don't believe everything that's told me by a patient sitting in that chair.

Now the woman who sat there this morning—I told you she had given all those nods of the head.

In the first interview, I had asked her if she had more than one love affair outside the home, and she freely confessed that she had a number of affairs. But she continued to mislead me about her problems and finally I told her, "I've done everything to get a statement of the problem." Let me see your driver's license." She was reluctant, but she got it out and showed it to me. I said, "So your driver's license expires within the next week. You're really afraid to go down there and take the exam. Now will you please tell me why you're afraid to go down and take the exam. Certainly you must know I *know* what your problem is, because I got out that information about your driver's license. Now take out of your handbag your real problem—whiskey." *(Erickson laughs)*

Today I began telling her anecdotes about patients. She found them interesting. She empathized with the one woman who kept coming to me for a problem about being fearful at her work.

I told her a series of stories and she told me a series of stories in return. All of a sudden she realized that every one of her anecdotes had a common denominator. Then she recognized that the common denominator in her anecdotes was the same common denominator in my anecdotes. *(Erickson laughs)*

Z: Setting up the conditions so that she can spontaneously come to an understanding.

E: Uh-huh. I'll give you some fictitious anecdotes—you're not entitled to know the real ones.

Three of her friends started building new homes. At the same time she and her husband did. Another woman came into the situation and ruined the three marriages.

Another good friend was encountered by a woman she knew. She's not really likeable. [*(to Zeig)* Which means she's attractive but not likeable.] And then one of her friends had his marriage broken up by this woman.

*(to Zeig)* The other woman; the common denominator in the stories was—the other woman. In other words, her marriage is threatened. That's how I knew about her having an affair.

She said, "I know my husband offered me a book on sex and laughed at me because I wouldn't read it. I hid it in my desk drawer and haven't looked at it since." I said, "Yes. You underestimate your own personal value."

That's her problem. It isn't a phobia of flying in a plane. She didn't want to go back to the state where she and her husband are building a new home. She said she was afraid to get on the plane. I knew damned well she wasn't afraid of getting on a plane. She just wasn't going to admit to herself that she was fearful that maybe she was not adequate sufficiently for her husband. She's never dared to admit to herself that she feels inferior.

She's going to fly home next Friday and plans to enjoy the ride. She doesn't know it; she made up her mind without knowing it. She came in to see me today, hoping to tell me.

After all this came out, she said, "On the way back from California, I almost got into an accident on the freeway. It's horrible driving a car. It's such a lovely day for sailing in the air." Her husband had the business of flying, so yesterday she thought it was a lovely day to go up on a balloon flight. If she had a real phobia for being up in the air, she wouldn't think it was a lovely day to be in a plane. I had to take two hours with her today when I saw that she was really spiraling in on herself.

Erickson returns to the story of today's patient. He indicates how he used anecdotes to guide associations by returning story for story until the patient recognized "the common denominator" in his stories. He was meeting her at her level and respecting her unrecognized need to withhold information. Simultaneously, he was establishing an environment for change, and timing his therapy so his direct confrontation about low self-esteem would be effective.

Next, Erickson returns to the theme of pattern-predictable behavior by discussing his son-in-law, Dave.

E: Now, did you read that reprint? (*Erickson had seen to it that I was given the reprint of his article entitled "A Field Investigation by Hypnosis of Sound Loci Importance in Human Behavior"* [1973] ).

Z: I looked through the reprint and I read it before, too. It came out in the last issue of the *American Journal of Clinical Hypnosis*.

E: Uh-huh. I had to write the first case in 1929; the second in 1940, and third in 1968. I had everything down in rough form. I wrote the polished paper just last year.

Z: I can't understand how you ever came to the conclusion to use the sound locus idea with that third gentleman.

E: That was purely serendipitous. I had to demonstrate to Dr. Hackett that I could induce a trance in a way that didn't say "trance," that didn't say anything. And everybody's had that experience of sound loci.

When my blue-eyed daughter (*Betty Alice Elliott*) got through reading that account and she said, "Daddy, this is just nauseating. When I think of the things I did when I was a schoolgirl, I just get sick."

Her husband was a Lieutenant-Colonel in the Air Force. Response to sound is one of the things you have to learn to control if you want to be a jet pilot.

It also explains the way he drives a car. My daughter didn't mind it until the first baby arrived. They were taking the baby out to the car with them to go out and she said, "Dave, without delay, you're buying a second car. And hereafter the baby and I go in one car and you follow behind me." And so, she drives carefully, properly, and he flies behind in perfect formation. (*laughs*) They were coming from Nevada—it was a straight highway there, and she said, "I wonder how well he's flying in formation. So I'll weave the car back and forth." He followed and never noticed that she was deliberately weaving. (*Erickson laughs*)

Dave couldn't hear her when she would yell at him, "Stop the car—it's time to eat." He was just hearing the engine; he was focused on it. When you fly a one-engine jet plane at 60,000 feet, you have to listen to the engine and hear it. You've got to know the exact position of the plane in relationship just to yourself. You have to know whether you are flying with the plane on its side, or bottom side up, or on the other side. You've got to know the position of the plane in relationship to yourself, and the sound of the engine.

Now he's a safety officer. My daughter thought it was fun to drive the lead car and look in the rearview mirror and watch him fly in formation behind her. She tried putting on the brakes suddenly—he put them on equally suddenly. He flies in perfect formation—and it's comfortable. He *knows* he's in perfect formation. And what the lead car does is all right; he just sees to it that he duplicates its lead. He knew what that paper was about.

As a kid I was curious about the locus of sounds—listening

in all different directions. And Hackett thought you have to have a stereotyped induction: "Relax. Your eyes are closing. Your hand is lifting higher and higher. Your lids are closing more and more." All that patter and verbiage doesn't mean anything.

You create a situation in which a patient goes into a trance, and it isn't important that they know they're in a trance. The important thing is for you to know. If they want to tell you they haven't been in a trance, for your own interest you can dispute them, but only for your interest.

I can think of a man who said, "In two weeks' time, I've got to go to Boston by air. When it comes to airplanes, I freeze. I've tried to board a commercial plane several times, but I lose control of my muscles, I get paralyzed—I get afraid. I've tried to get into a private plane, but I can't. I have a history of thousands of hours in a plane. I know how to fly one. I've got to go to Boston, but I haven't been able to get on a plane for five years. My partner does all the travel. Now I've got to go. Will you put me in a trance and remove my phobia for planes?" I told him, "Yes."

I spent a little over an hour. He said, "That was most unsatisfactory. I wasn't in a real trance. I could hear the cars outside, the birds, the bus, pick-up trucks, big trucks, sports cars, the Ford and the Chevrolets. I couldn't avoid hearing different cars. How about giving me another session?" I said, "You were in a sufficiently deep trance. I don't think I should give you another session." He said, "I don't think so. Give me another session." I said, "All right, you can have another session. But when you leave today, I want from you, first of all, an absolute promise that you will do *nothing* to correct your problem as you see it. Absolutely nothing to correct your problem as you see it."

He came back for a second session—it was a failure again. I didn't tell him about the two sirens that went by in the first trance. He went to Boston.

Another patient told me, "Today is Monday, and Thursday I have to go to Dallas or I lose my job. [*This case is reported in more detail and with different emphasis in Zeig, 1980a, p. 64.*] I was in a plane accident in 1962—no real damage was done to the plane; nobody was injured. I continued to fly on the plane, but progressively I resorted to other forms of travel—trains, cars, buses. I used up my vacation time, and my sick leave time that way. Now my boss says I've got to fly a plane. It's been a year since I dared to."

She gave me additional information. "As long as the plane is on the ground, I'm all right. I can taxi to the end of the runway and from the end of the runway to the airport, but once that plane lifts off, I go into a state of absolute terror. I shudder the whole time until I'm into a state of physical exhaustion."

I did the therapy with her. After she got back from Dallas, she called me from the Phoenix airport and told me the trip was fantastic. I had four of my Ph.D. students coming that evening for a class, so I had her show up. I also asked the previous man to come. She told the students how she had come to me and what I did. I had put her into a trance. After the therapy, I had her board the plane from Phoenix. On the way to El Paso, the first stop, she wondered uncomfortably if her fear of flying would return. She said, "When we reached El Paso, there was a 20-minute stopover. I got off the plane, went to a secluded place in the airport. I sat down and told myself, "Count to 20 and go into a trance. Tell yourself exactly what Dr. Erickson told you to do and come back from the trance when you count from 20 to one." She did that and the rest of the trip was pleasurable.

I had her tell the story to the four students and the man, and then I said to her, "You think you told me your problem, don't you?" She said, "I did." "But you didn't tell me all of your problem." She said, "I did." "No. You've got some more problems. See if you can't think of some hampering fears that you have." "But I haven't any," she said. "Maybe I'd better help you. What about acrophobia?" She said, "What's that?" "Fear of heights." She said, "Oh, yes. When I got to Dallas, I went to that building with the outside elevator, and I rode comfortably all the way to the top and back down again. It's the first time I ever rode an elevator like that."

I said, "All right, that's part of your problem. What's another part?" She said, "I don't know. There isn't any other part." I said, "I *know* that there is another part to your problem. Now is there anything odd or peculiar which you do when you're driving?" She said, "Oh, yes. Whenever I have to go over a bridge in a car, I shut my eyes and cower down. I'm afraid to cross the bridge."

The man jumped up and said, "I can think of something." I said, "Yes? Tell them how you broke your promise to me." He said, "All I did was go downtown and take that outside elevator to the top floor. That had nothing to do with my problem. Then I went to the airport and taxied the plane to the end of the runway, but I couldn't lift off." I said, "That's right, but you did enjoy part of your trip to Boston and back."

Z: I'm confused. You told him not to do anything about his problem as he saw it.

E: *(overlapping)* . . . as he understood it. He had ridden an elevator for the first time in his life, and he had taxied a plane down to the end of the runway.

You didn't listen when I told you his problem. He couldn't *board* a commercial plane. He just became paralyzed. He couldn't walk *into* a plane. He couldn't climb *into* a plane. He thought it was fear of flying. I let him keep on thinking it was *fear* of flying. *(Erickson laughs)* Therefore, he wasn't doing anything to correct it. And, therefore, he could have it corrected by the hypnosis, which he thought was unsatisfactory. *(Erickson laughs)*

Z: And he corrected it.

E: He didn't correct it, but I had corrected it.

And the girl, what was her fear? It wasn't of plane flying, she could taxi to the end of the runway, she could taxi from the end of the runway to the airport. Therefore, she was not afraid of being in a plane. She just thought she was. My therapy was that I told her, "Before I will do any therapy, first I've got to find out if you're a good hypnotic subject. Let's see if you can develop a trance." She could. So I awakened her and said, "Now, listen. You want therapy. I can give you therapy. You don't really understand your problem, or you wouldn't have your problem. I know the right way to correct it. I want you to promise me absolutely, without question, without any limitations, that you will do anything and everything that I say, whether good or bad. You're an attractive young woman. I am a man. Being confined to a wheelchair doesn't really mean too much. I want an absolute promise that you will do anything and everything that I ask you to do." She hesitated and then said, "Nothing you could ask me to do would be worse than what happens to me on a plane. I promise you absolutely."

What she didn't know was, she could not stand to be in an enclosed space where she could see no support underneath. And neither could the man. What I had to get him over was his fear of boarding a plane. What I had to get her over was the fear of being absolutely committed.

Z: Absolutely committed?

E: Because you are committed when you are in a plane in the air. You have nothing to say about anything. The pilot's flying the plane. You can't do anything—you can't get off; you can't guide it—you're just committed.

Z: So when she put her trust in you and made a commitment to you. . . .

E: (*overlapping*) When she made an absolute commitment to me, she found out that she could live through a commitment.

Z: I see.

E: That's how I knew she must have a bridge phobia and an elevator phobia.

Z: And the car going over the bridge with somebody else driving—I see.

E: And most people will try to analyze that phobia in other terms.

Z: So you generally disregard the person's complaint?

E: I listen to the meaningfulness of what they describe. She said she could taxi to the end of the runway and taxi back to the airport comfortably. But when the plane was airborne, she shuddered. And he said he became paralyzed and couldn't walk onto a plane; the fear of getting into a plane, that's where his discomfort lay. I let him think he continued to have a fear—that I was unsuccessful. And he certainly didn't understand the real meaning of the ride in the elevator.

Z: And that's why you would be sure—he would test that out.

E: I knew he'd test that out. He'd still think he had his problem.
   And too many people listen to the problem and they don't hear
   what the patient *isn't* saying *(Erickson laughs)* when they should.
   That's the really important thing.
   *(Erickson calls the main house and asks Mrs. Erickson to come out
   and get him.)*
E: I'm through for the day.
Z: O.K.
E: You're at liberty to do what you wish. I have an eleven-o'clock
   appointment tomorrow and a one-o'clock appointment tomor-
   row. At noon, I'll go in my house and probably take a small
   lunch, and then come out and see my one o'clock. At two o'clock,
   I'll see you. Now you'd better read that article on my technique
   by Haley and Weakland and see the way I structured things.
Z: The "Trance Induction with Commentary," right? (Erickson,
   Haley, and Weakland, 1959) O.K.
E: Because when you're dealing with patients, you're saying something
   and mentioning something the meaning of which will become
   apparent to the patient maybe in half an hour, maybe next week.
Z: Seeding.
E: And the best way for me to find out if you have brothers, and not
   let you know it, is to start bragging about my brother.

## SUMMARY

In this day's session, Erickson told three cases of phobias. I do not
think that this was accidental.

Prior to my visit, Erickson knew of my trepidation about meeting
him. I had met two of his colleagues, Robert Pearson, M.D., and Kay
Thompson, D.D.S., at a professional meeting that I attended just
before visiting Erickson. Subsequently, Pearson called Erickson and
told him about me (Pearson, 1982).

Through his phobia stories, Erickson was empathizing with my
unstated fears. Moreover, there was a positive outcome; in each case,
the phobia was unexpectedly resolved. In a similar fashion, I was
being subtly directed towards resolution of my own fears.

In talking about phobias, Erickson was working to guide my associations. He was not directly telling me what to think. Rather, he was creating subtle pressure to think in specific directions. Take the example he provided of getting a person to talk about his brother by talking about one's own brother. At first I didn't understand the importance of this technique. However, I soon understood that guiding associations was a cornerstone of Erickson's method. Psychotherapy often occurs at the level of preconscious associations, the same level at which problems are generated. A patient's thinking can be gradually changed by the guiding of associations. Through this method, change becomes more patient-initiated.

Let us examine some of the other themes from the session. Erickson stressed common-sense approaches to create a climate for patient-based change. He used drama to enhance the effectiveness of his method. On one hand, he could be indirect (one-step removed). However, he could set limits and be firm and confrontive. Observation and utilization of minimal cues were of utmost value, as was understanding the patient from within the patient's frame of reference. Erickson also emphasized the positive. He would look for resources in the reality context that could be identified and developed. Where others paid lip service to the importance of patient strengths, Erickson showed how a therapist could really use them.

In the next two days, Erickson will tell stories directed to personal and professional themes such as, "trust your unconscious," "be playful and flexible in therapy and life," and "face fears directly." He will again emphasize predictability in behavior, and unchangeable patterns. Also, he will tell stories that are family-oriented, directed to traditional values and self-reliance. Perhaps some of his method was directed to help me at my particular state of development. At the time I was a young adult looking forward to the transition of having my own family.

## DAY TWO, DECEMBER 4, 1973

Erickson is obviously in pain. He has difficulty transferring himself from his wheelchair to his office chair. His voice is weak.

E: I forgot to tell you one thing yesterday. Timing is very important.

When you're speaking to a patient, and you want them to recognize a common denominator or you want to stimulate a recollection on their part, you try to time your utterance so that you hit them with what you want to say at the exact right moment.

Now, I'm going to be slow today. I had to time things with yesterday's patient very carefully, and when you time yourself, you build tension. As a result of yesterday, I couldn't help tensing my muscles so I had innumerable muscle contractions and severe pain all night long. You see, I've got spinal arthritis, riticulitis, myositis, tenosynovitis and gout. My hands, my knees, my sciatic nerve, my leg, my right foot, my head were in an awkward position. I've got a stiff neck. So I'll be slowed up today.

Now that you've met me, you finally figured out the answer to that troubled question you put to Pearson and Thompson.

Z: Which question was that?

E: What will I do when I meet him?

Z: *(laughing)* It was a *very* troubled question. When I talked to Dr. Pearson that day I was scared.

E: Of what? I'm in a wheelchair. I can't chase you. I haven't got the muscles to throw you around.

Z: *(obviously moved)* Dr. Erickson, I'm so incredibly impressed by you.

E: Well, the only thing I can say about that is I finally managed to impress my kids.

Z: I'm sorry?

E: I finally managed to impress my kids. They've always considered me a bit backward. A bit mentally retarded.

Z: You're an incredible person.

E: No, I'm a curious person.

Z: The opportunity to spend these few hours with you are so meaningful for me that I really don't have words to describe it.

E: Well, I'm just another bozo on the road of life.

Z: *(laughs)*

E: And now, what have you done since I saw you yesterday?

Z: Spent some time going over the tape of our session.

E: How clear is my speech?

Z: Very clear. As a matter of fact, I could understand you clearer when I listened to the tape. I also spent some time reading through the *Trance Induction with Commentary*, although I haven't quite finished that.

I have a question about one thing you said yesterday. When you were doing therapy with the woman with the phobia you said, "I'm a man and I'm in a wheelchair and you're a woman." Why did you present those ideas that way? Why did you emphasize your being a man and her being a woman?

E: She is an attractive, married woman. Everything from the best to the worst. The worst threat for an attractive, young, married woman would have to be sex.

Z: So there was a definite seductiveness to your suggestion.

E: Not seductive, a sexual threat. Far removed from airplanes. And even though I'm physically confined to a wheelchair, I could still ask her to undress. I could still ask to play with her breasts; ask her to play with me. I could still make sexual remarks. I wanted her to feel hopelessly entrapped, like she was when the plane lifts off the ground.

You need to treat patients within the framework of their difficulty. She didn't know what the framework of her difficulty was. I knew what it was—a fear of complete entrapment where she had no control of any sort. And although my male patient thought about his difficulty as being on a plane, I knew it wasn't. That's the importance of actually hearing what your patients say.

Another thing—we all have nonverbal language. When I took my first job in Worcester, Massachusetts, the clinical director said, "Erickson, you've got a bad limp. So have I. I don't know what caused yours, but I got mine in World War I. I had 29 operations for osteomyelitis in my leg, and I've learned from experience that a physical difficulty is a tremendous asset in psychiatry. You draw out the maternal instinct in women; they want to help you. No matter how psychotic they are, you do appeal to their maternal instincts, only they don't know it. As for the men, you're not a threat—you're not a rival to them. You're just a cripple. So you've got it made in psychiatry."

The next bit of advice I'm going to give you is this: Keep a straight face. Now how many young people are curious about sex? There are a lot of unanswered questions. If you're not afraid in talking about sex, if you're not rude about it, if you don't try to make a subject of humor out of it, if you treat it as you would a question of blood pressure or pulse, they'll look upon you as a good person in whom to confide.

Listen to every tentative question about sex: People will tell you things. And attend to the nonverbal communication as well as the verbal. In doing so, convey to them your willingness to discuss anything. And as you gain experience, you'll probably know more than they do and that helps them to confide in you, as long as they think you know more than they do. "He already knows it, so why not talk."

Z: By talking generally—being vague?

E: No, not vague. "Of course, I know what's been going on recently."

Z: I see.

E: It's an accusation; it implies I do know. Maybe I don't. But as long as I do know, you might as well talk. (*Erickson's next patient arrives.*) (*to the patient*) Come in. (*After he sees the patient, the session continues.*) This last patient came to me with a particular problem. Actually, she has a defective self-image. There was a certain rhythm of lip. . . .

Z: Rhythm of her lip movements?

E: I noticed an unnecessary rhythm of lip movement. I noticed an acceleration of her pulse.

Z: In her neck?

E: Yes. She had a miniskirt on. I noticed a rhythmical movement of her inner thigh muscle. So I told her she had some sexual conflicts.

Z: And how did she react to that?

E: She said that she certainly had and asked how I knew. I told her how I knew. She was pleased that I brought it up, because she wasn't willing to tell me. She didn't want me to know when she came in. But her unconscious mind wanted me to know, so I told her. And I didn't ask for information.

She wants to come in next week and I told her, "Aren't you a bit impatient?" She said, "That's my failing." (*Erickson laughs*) She *knows* she's too impatient.

Z: Did you agree to see her next week?

E: No. I gave her an appointment two weeks from now. I asked if that was all right, and her head made a perseverative nod without her knowing it.

Z: Confirmation.

E: Watch your patients and see what they're doing and saying, verbally and nonverbally.

Z: Sometimes you choose to react to an unconscious movement indirectly. In this case, you made a direct interpretation.

E: It depends on whether you have a fairly open personality, or a fearful personality. This girl is fairly open, and she's impatient. The first thing to correct is her impatience. I didn't give her an appointment as soon as she wanted one. And she touched me carefully on the shoulder when she left.

Z: Meaning what?

E: "I like you."

Z: A related question. Sometimes you choose to make responses that are geared to be outside of the patient's awareness.

E: Uh-huh. One young woman told me she had a fear of flying in a plane. I didn't think she had. I told her she didn't have a fear of planes. Last year she married a German flight engineer. She developed a fear of flying to Germany. She was 32 years old; it was her first marriage. She was very attractive, very likeable. Her German husband spoke English with scarcely a trace of an accent. He was obviously in love with her. Her husband had to go back to Germany for job reasons; he had completed additional technical training here at the air base. After he returned to Germany to confirm his job, he came back to get her.

I told her I could prove she didn't have a fear of planes. I had her board a plane to Tucson. She was fearful all the way there; the stewardess had to hold her hand and comfort her. She was so exhausted she had to stay over one day in Tucson. She was hysterical all the way back.

She came in to her appointment and asked where next was I going to make her fly. If she had a true fear, she wouldn't come in and ask where next would I make her fly. So I told her, "You aren't weaned. You've struggled to stay with your parents. You never really left your parents."

I got a card from her recently. It was written in German. It said, "With Greetings from our *home* to your house." *(Erickson laughs.)* A house isn't a home. It's merely a house to her. Her parents live in a house in Arizona. And *home* is now Germany *(laughs)*. Such a little thing. "Grüsse unseren Heim Ihren Haus." Reducing a home in Phoenix to a mere house, and making Germany home. *(Erickson laughs)* Such a brief statement. All you have to know is the difference between a house and a home. She could have written "von Hausen zu Hausen," but she said, "Heim zu Hausen." Home to House. That told everything. Also, a true phobic wouldn't come in and say, "Where's the next place you're going to make me fly."

Z: Which was hooking on to you as a parent.

E: Uh-huh.

Z: And you picked up on how she related to you to make your confrontation.

E: That she wasn't weaned, even though she was 32-years-old. Now why bother about analyzing her childhood? You're not going to change the past. You can enlighten them about the past, but what good is mere education about the past. You're living today, tomorrow, the next week, the next month. And that's what counts. I tell teenagers, "When do you want to be happy—now, in your short, teen years, your brief twenties, or would you prefer to be happy the last 50 years of your life." *(Erickson laughs)*

Z: That socks it to 'em.

E: That's right. It *is* a short teenage period and a brief 20s. The last 50 years of their life is a long, long time.

Z: If it's not possible to sit in with you the next patient you have, would it be possible to tape it and go over it?

E: Psychiatric patients would think, "What in hell does that psychiatrist want to know about me?" To tape record can be an awful affront. When I see a new patient, I don't know what that patient is like. I'm not going to offer a threat. It's your loss—the patient's gain. The patient wants a safe room, and this highly individual, purely personal room conveys safety.

Erickson takes a break and then returns. He picks up by discussing a case in which he told a procrastinating female patient to "skate or get off the ice." She could have another appointment when she demonstrated commitment by doing a week of volunteer work.

E: If she does a whole week's work, she can have another appointment with me.

Z: But she has to do one week's work, and that will be the skating.

E: It's got to be a whole week of hard work, not an intention to volunteer to do something.

Z: That's been the problem—the intentions. "I'll try, I'll try," but nothing happens.

E: She just doesn't get around to trying (*laughs*).

And her therapist, whom she had previously seen, had been patiently telling her, week after week, "You really ought to try." Well, she got her ultimatum now. She paid hard cash for it. I'm not going to be a time waster.

Z: Was that a hypnotic session? Did you use formal trance?

E: You don't give your patient a chance to tell you, "You gave me a hypnotic suggestion and it didn't work." (*Erickson laughs*) That way, they can blame me. I give them suggestions, and they themselves have to take the responsibility.

Z: So you are presenting ideas and suggestions outside of their conscious awareness.

E: (*as if talking to the patient*) And you don't like wasting your time at home on temporary alimony for the next few years. You keep promising yourself that you'll prepare yourself for a job. You haven't even left the house to visit the zoo, the Heard Museum, the art gallery, or the Botanical Gardens. You've done nothing except say, "I really ought to do something."

Z: Presenting it to her so there's no way she can deny it and she has to face reality.

E: Just a cold, gently worded, appraisal of the bare facts. (*Erickson laughs*) I told her she had to skate or get off the ice. She said, "My former therapist told me that at least 50 times." I said, "All right, I'll put it to you another way. Either shit or get off the pot. I'm saying that *once*." (*Erickson laughs*)

Z: Not like 50 other times. Okay. I have a question. You don't choose to see people on a rigid time schedule like many other therapists. The people who have come here have come 10 minutes, five minutes early, even half an hour, and you see them right then.

E: If I'm available. Why should I make them wait?

Z: The issue of not being a threatening figure seems very important.

E: They came to see me for help. If I don't have anything demanding my attention right now, let's start. Freedom. Too many psychotherapists have scheduled patients for three months in advance. They live 50 minutes at a time, and rest 10 minutes. It's a ritualistic, unbreakable pattern. That's not practicing psychotherapy. Psychotherapy should teach people how to live, not how to follow a rigid, demanding schedule.

My patients understand if I happen to have an opportunity to go somewhere on the day of their appointment, there will be another day in the week. We're not going to be tied down; I'm going to have freedom in life, so should they. There should be reasonable considerations of one another.

I should have the freedom to make decisions. And you should have the freedom to accept whatever I'm willing to give you.

Z: Or reject it.

E: You won't get more than I'm willing to give you.

Z: A lot of leeway and a lot of firmness.

E: That's right. An understanding that's firm. Some young woman says, "I want very much to kiss you." You tell her, "That's your wish; I'm not strong enough to resist you, but I don't have to participate."

Z: Has that situation happened to you?

E: Oh, yes.

Z: And what's been the response after you've said something like that?

E: The response has been one of increased respect. I remember one startling incident. A woman rushed in from the street one day, a stranger to Mrs. Erickson. She put her arms around me and kissed me, and kissed me, and kissed me. Mrs. Erickson wondered what was going on. Finally, the woman released me and said, "I'm so glad you made me give that promise. Thank you so much." I said, "I, too, am glad you gave that promise. I heard the radio. I know what happened, too."

(*to Zeig*) I made her promise to divorce her husband, and refuse to either ride in the car with him or let her daughter ride in the car with him. I made her promise that in her husband's presence. She got a divorce. He went and bought a new car. He said to his wife, "I just bought this new car—how about taking a ride with me around the block?" She started to get in the car, but didn't. She remembered her promise. When she didn't get in and refused to let her daughter get in, he said, "All right, I'll go over to my girlfriend's." He left happily for his girlfriend. Then he got intoxicated and started speeding. The girlfriend was killed in the auto wreck. He was paralyzed from the neck down. I had judged him correctly. His ex-wife was in her car with the radio on when she heard the announcement.

Z: And came over here.

E: Came over realizing how close she had come to death. She didn't give time for me to explain things to Mrs. Erickson.

This strange woman came dashing into the house, going through that performance. She had only been a block away from my house when the announcement came on. So it didn't take long to get to the house. I listened to the radio thinking I was fortunate to have warned his ex-wife not to ride with him. I did it in front of her husband. I was being aboveboard. They heard what I said. There was no anger when I said it. It was said in a matter-of-fact way.

I was perfectly willing to tell him and his wife, "Your wife wants you to keep on having women friends—that's her privilege. I don't think it's good for her, and I don't think it's good for you, but you may enjoy it. I doubt if your wife does. I don't see how it prolongs a marriage. I think it's more likely to lead to divorce." He didn't take my advice. I said my say. There was no anger, resentment or hostility that they could fight against. They had to listen to me.

Z: You provide a tremendous amount of respect and caring for the people that you see.

E: That's right.

Z: On many different levels.

E: That's right. It's an easier, much more comfortable way of living.

One of my daughters was in 8th grade. She came to the table with dirty hands one Sunday. We were having her favorite food, chicken, for dinner, and I started to serve.

I told her, "When someone comes to the table for dinner, one comes with clean hands." She looked at her hands. They were very dirty. So she jumped up and dashed in the kitchen, went to the kitchen faucet, and came out shaking her hands dry. She sat down and eyed the chicken with a hopeful look.

I said, "One washes dirty dishes in the kitchen; dirty hands are washed in the bathroom." She went rushing into the bathroom, washed her hands, came out shaking them dry and sat down, looking at that chicken. I said, "Still sorry. When one washes one's hands, one dries them with a towel."

So she went to the bathroom, washed her hands, came out, dried them very elaborately, went back to the bathroom, hung up the towel, came back and sat down and looked at me with an expression of "I've done everything you've said."

I said, "When one washes one's hands, one notices whether or not the wrists are dirty and the forearms are dirty. And if they are, those too are washed." She really scrubbed down. (*Erickson laughs.*) She sat down. I said, "It's now time for second helpings, and since I haven't given you a first helping, I don't know how to give you a second helping. Now, you are at liberty to go to the refrigerator and take out anything that Mother didn't prepare." So she took out a bottle of milk, went to the breadbox and took out the bread and had bread and milk. There's no reason to go hungry. Leftovers, no. Carrots, lettuce and celery, yes. Mother didn't prepare them.

Z: So you're saying in a very firm way that you're not going to allow that kind of outburst.

E: Letting the child reap what has been sown. She shouldn't have come to the table with dirty hands. (*Erickson laughs*) She knew that as well as I did. I merely made a general observation. She knew to whom it fit.

Z: I see.

E: Once one of my sons defiantly said, "I am not going to eat any of that stuff." I said, "Certainly not. You are not old enough.

You're not big enough. You're not strong enough." And his mother very defensively said, "He is too big enough. He is too strong enough." *(Erickson laughs)*

His mother and I had a debate about it. I was hard to convince. My son was hoping his mother would win. And now he pulls the same stunt on his kids. *(laughs)* Why shouldn't you do it that way?

Z: Setting it up so that the choice is theirs.

E: It is their choice. I have heard my kids say, "Well, I forgot to do something." The siblings reply, "You had no business forgetting it. I wonder what daddy will think of." *(Erickson laughs)* And he or she will say, "I think I had better get it done right now." *(Erickson laughs)*

Z: Like forgetting a chore around the house.

E: Because what daddy thinks of is so unexpected.

Z: It might be worse.

E: It always is. *(laughs)*

One of my daughters was going to introduce her boyfriend to us at Christmas time. He was 6' 4". The first time he had been west of Chicago was shortly before Christmas. Although he passed through Tucson, he was too timid to call us up. So I told my daughter, "When you bring 'Chicken Little' here over Christmas vacation, I will greet him with a machete and ask him what his intentions are." *(laughs)* She said, "Don't do that, that's terrible." I said, "Well, I can think of something worse." *(laughs)*

One of my youngest sons gathered various friends to the house to announce his engagement. He has got a very wry sense of humor. Very unexpected. Difficult to catch on to, but you always catch on to it. He told a shaggy dog story: "I had you come to this house because I had something very important to say to you. Some day, I think it was last March—maybe it was May—anyway, I was driving the car. . . ." He kept on going off on tangents. At the end of half an hour he decided on a tangent that said he was announcing his engagement. I said, "Now if we had some rye bread, we could have ham on rye."

Practical jokes are a way of life with us. Psychotherapy should follow that order.

When Bert *(Erickson's oldest son)* was living in Michigan, we were living in Arizona. *(This case is also reported in Rosen, 1982a, p. 218.)* He got out of the Marines in June, and he wrote us a letter, "Have to close now. I have got to see Delores." The next week there was another letter, "Had a nice dinner with Delores." That's all. Another letter said, "Perhaps you would like to see some snapshots of Delores."

He carried on the same correspondence with my parents. In September, we got a nice letter, "I wonder if Grandma and Grandpa would like Delores?" In October, he said he had a way that Grandma and Grandpa could meet Delores. Later in October, he decided to have Thanksgiving with Grandma and Grandpa and Delores.

At 1:00 a.m. Thanksgiving day—it was very cold in Milwaukee—he knocked on my parents' door. Bert has the capacity to be cross-eyed and stand pigeon-toed, his arms hanging down in a helpless fashion. And he has a sickly grin on his face. You want to slap him because it is so disgusting, that sickly grin. My father opened the door. Bert came in. My father said, "Where's Delores?" Bert stood pigeon-toed, cross-eyed, arms hanging down, with that sickly grin on his face and said, "I had trouble getting Delores on the plane." "Trouble, what do you mean?" "She isn't properly dressed." "Where is she?" "She is outside. She isn't properly dressed." My mother said, "I am going to go get a bathrobe." [Commandingly] my father said, "Bring that girl in." Bert came in carrying a great big box. He said [weakly], "This is the only way that I could get her on the plane. She wasn't properly dressed." My father commandingly said, "Open it." Slowly, Bert opened it. Delores was inside—one goose and one turkey—both named Delores. And Grandma and Grandpa liked Delores. *(Erickson laughs)* A long distance joke.

Z: And well planned out and well set up.

E: Betty Alice had been traveling through Europe and teaching school in Detroit. I was lecturing there. She came to attend the lecture and we went to dinner in the hotel. The waitress came. My daughter ordered, and said she would like to see the wine list. She inspected the card. I ordered a daquiri; so did Mrs. Erickson.

The waitress looked uncertainly at Betty Alice. She asked, "Could I have your identification please." The waitress was very polite. Betty Alice had to prove her age six different ways. Finally, she said, "I guess it will be all right for you to order a drink." Betty Alice said, "A Rosy Deacon, please." The waitress looked a bit bewildered and went to the bar. She came back and said, "The bartender said there is no such drink." Betty Alice said, "Bring me a Pale Preacher." The waitress went back to the bartender, came back and said, "The bartender said there is no such drink." Betty Alice said, "Will you please call the manager." The manager of the hotel came to our table. Betty Alice said, "I ordered a Rosy Deacon and your waitress was told by the bartender that they didn't have the drink, so I was going to compromise and said I would have a Pale Preacher. The bartender refused to make a Pale Preacher. Now, if you don't mind, sir, don't you think you ought to buy a Bartender's Guide for your bartender?" He said, "We have one." He went back and the bartender looked it up and the manager said, "How do you make a Rosy Deacon?" She told him. "How do you make a Pale Preacher." She told him. They looked at the Bartender's Guide; they wanted to make sure. *(Erickson laughs)* Any waitress that took so long to decide whether that 22-year-old girl was 21 or not could be used for a little harmless amusement.

Z: Uh-huh.

E: And the manager had a Rosy Deacon made, and said, "I'm going to try it too." He sat down and he had a Rosy Deacon. Then he ordered a Pale Preacher. Then he told Betty Alice, "I am going to have those two drinks added to our list," and he laughed.

I went to an oyster bar in New Orleans. I told the waiter, "Bring me a dozen raw oysters, and while I am eating those, prepare a second dozen." He said, "These are Mississippi oysters and they are pretty large." I said, "I know. Just prepare the second dozen." I ate the first dozen. He brought the second dozen. I said, "While I am eating these, prepare a third dozen." He said, "Sir, are you out of your mind?" I said, "No. I don't want to be out of oysters." I ordered, under protest, five dozen oysters. I ate 60 oysters. He looked at me and said, incredulously,

"Sixty Mississippi oysters!" "Yes," I said, "and 60 birthdays."
(*Erickson laughs*) Why shouldn't I have 60 oysters on my 60th
birthday?

Z: How many are you going to have tomorrow?

E: My wife is buying two additional cans, plus the two cans that
we have.

Z: How old will you be tomorrow?

E: Seventy-two.

Z: Happy Birthday.

E: In the East, I went into a hotel dining room. I was handed
a menu in French. I protested I didn't read French. The waiter
with a very thick accent said that he would help me. I pointed
to an item and asked, "What's that." He explained what it was,
but it was very difficult to understand him. I pointed to other
things. I didn't let him know that I knew what they were. Finally,
I said, "Bring me a glass of cracked ice." He looked puzzled,
but he brought it. I said, "Now bring me a bottle of French
dressing." He was even more puzzled. I poured some French
dressing on the cracked ice. I said, "Now, put this in the garbage,
will you please." He said (without a trace of an accent), "Yes,
sir." (*Erickson laughs*) He knew that I knew his accent was phony.
Why quarrel with a waiter. He wants to put something over on
you, why not enjoy it.

A couple of years later, in Portland, Oregon, in a hotel dining
room, a waiter greeted me and said, "How do you do, Dr.
Erickson?" I said, "Well, I don't know you. But obviously you
know me." He said, "You will know me before the evening is
over." (*to Zeig*) I don't have a good memory for faces. (*continues*)
He brought my check. I paid the bill. He brought back the
change. I left the tip. And he thanked me with a very thick
French accent. (*Erickson laughs*) Then I knew him!

And with patients, you handle their problems in a similar way.

That woman who told me that she was sick and tired of being
so frightfully inhibited. Her mother's life had been one of complete inhibition by a hostile husband. She and her sisters had
patterned after their mother. They led inhibited lives. She wished
she would get over being inhibited. I told her she ought to get

off the ice or skate. That's what her other psychotherapist had said many times. "All right, I will say it to you once. Get off the pot, or shit." *(Erickson laughs)*

I hit her hard. And that was a much better way than trying to reeducate her about her inhibitions. And now she can't think about her past without viewing it in those crude terms. It's not so easy anymore to say, "I am inhibited." She has got to think, "Get off the pot or. . . ." *(Erickson laughs)* When an inhibited person gets that kind of statement, they have to face it by that name thereafter.

The funny things that patients will tell you. One patient came in and said, "I was dining with so and so who is also a patient of yours, and she embarrassed me terribly. I could scarcely control my embarrassment. While we were at the table, she said that she was flat-busted." I said, "One can be embarrassed by being flat-busted. *(Erickson laughs)* And in two different ways."

Some weeks later, she was at the country club and found herself in an embarrassing position. She said, "I was flat-assed broke." *(Erickson laughs)* But to her it was the other woman who had said the vulgar thing, "flat-busted." She was now saying, "Flat-assed broke."

A psychiatrist from another state who was a student of mine sent a patient he had been working with for three years. I took her name, address, telephone number. I asked her her problem. I got all the general data.

I said, "Madam, you are a woman. I am a man. When I look at a woman, I am entitled to see bumps in a certain place in her body. If you haven't got them, you can go downtown and buy some falsies. Buy them any size you wish, small, medium, or jumbo-sized. The next time you walk into this office, I want to see the falsies on your chest." She was wearing a very tight blouse. She had no breasts.

She showed up the next session wearing medium-sized falsies. We talked about various things, about her widowship. She had been happily married. Her husband died and left her an adequate amount of money. About a month later, I saw her psychiatrist who said, "What on earth did you do to that woman? She came home almost as soon as she reached Phoenix. She is happy and she is well adjusted and she won't tell me what you did for her." Here was a 50-year-old woman who wished all her life to have bumps and I told her, "Go get them." *(Erickson laughs)* It was all the therapy she needed.

Z: Were there any clues that you had?

E: That rigid, strained behavior, and that blouse was much too tight. So why not sock it to her on the basis that, "I am a man, you are a woman. And I as a man am entitled. . . ." It was my right! I didn't take up the question of whether she was entitled or ought to. I made it purely a matter of *my* right. She satisfied my rights and in the process took care of her rights without argument, without discussion.

Z: And in a wry way.

E: And in my way. Three years of therapy. I expressed it as my right. How are you going to dispute that and say it is wrong. It is incontestable. And since it was incontestable, she couldn't fight it. And so she helplessly did the right thing for herself. People really want to do the right thing *by themselves,* they are not going to let other people make them do it. *(Erickson laughs)* I could have talked myself silly for years telling her to wear falsies. And she could have argued. I said it was my right. It was not my right to know whether they were falsies or not, I was just entitled to see some bumps. *(Erickson laughs)*

Z: Presented in a way that she was trapped and could do nothing but something good for herself.

E: Except something good for her, under the guise of it being my right.

Z: Um-hmm.

E: Why shouldn't therapy be done that way instead of polite, dancing around the outside of a problem?

I think I had better go in the house. *(end of session)*

### DAY THREE, DECEMBER 5, 1973

As noted in the text, a number of cases discussed by Erickson on December 5, 1973, are already in print in other sources. Therefore, some cases have been summarized. However, because there are additional interesting elaborations and because it is interesting to study Erickson's process, some are also reported here.

Mrs. Erickson brought Dr. Erickson into the room. Erickson begins by discussing his treatment of John (see pp. 20-27) who that day had given Erickson a letter describing some of his feelings about Erickson and his personal therapy.

E: Well, I have been a godlike figure in this life. He has now recognized that I am human. It has been troubling me that I have been like a god to him. I have been trying to get him to realize that I was human without telling him to do that. Now I think that I have gotten it across to him. I think that the Lady of the House (*Mrs. Erickson*) is my successor.

Mrs. E: Dr. Erickson had an acute illness about two years ago and got over it quite rapidly, but I really have thought if it had been fatal, poor John, at that point, would have gone to a mental hospital. I think that letter was letting me know that he is catching on that his life expectancy is probably a good deal more than Dr. Erickson's is. (*When Dr. Erickson dies*) John will keep coming over on the same basis which is what I hope will happen.

E: And when you kick the bucket, I think if Roxie is in this neighborhood. . . .

Mrs. E: Oh, I think any of them would be accepted as a substitute, although I don't think he would feel that he would have to come over every day.

Well, I had better go back in. (*Mrs. Erickson leaves*)

Z: Did you make deliberate mistakes or do something to show him that you were human?

E: I didn't make mistakes. I have written a letter for Barney to a friend's dog in Puerto Rico—Muffin Woo Woo—I have written letters to Muffin and to Fritz and Jenny, my son's dogs. I wrote a whole series of more than 40 limericks for Barney. You see we had a basset hound that lived with us for 13 years who is now in the great boneyard up yonder, and he writes letters to "Earth Momma, Mrs. Erickson."

Z: I don't understand.

E: He is in the great boneyard up yonder—he is Ghost Roger, and he writes letters. They are signed "Ghost Roger."

Z: Who ghostwrites them?

E: I do. *(Zeig and Erickson laugh)*

E: And all of my kids were reared on White Tummy stories. "Once upon a time, there was a little frog with a green back and a white tummy. Because he had a white tummy and a green back, he was named White Tummy." My kids were all individuals and each of them demanded a different kind of series of adventures for White Tummy. So I made up stories to fit the needs of little children.

Then my blue-eyed daughter, after she was in the stage where her kids were demanding stories, said, "I can't make up stories. Why don't you do it?" So I have been writing White Tummy stories and my secretary types them with multiple carbon copies. They are sent to all the grandchildren. For example, White Tummy rides a time machine back into the past, and he discovers two little boys in a blackberry patch quarreling—Bert and Lance *(Erickson's oldest sons)*. And every sin that my kids committed in their youth, White Tummy relates.

Now Ghost Roger is also giving a family history. My son, Robert, from very early childhood was preoccupied with locks. He put a burglar alarm in his home because there are so many burglaries in Phoenix. One afternoon the alarm sounded and aroused the entire neighborhood. A woman called us up, and Betty called the police and met them at Robert's home. There were no burglars there. The alarm was ringing; the police searched the house. There was nothing missing. However, it was discovered that Robert had thoughtlessly allowed his doorlocks to be opened with a credit card.

Now Ghost Roger is writing about the newly arrived Ghost Pigeon and the Great Cooing Colt up yonder. And Ghost Pigeon is relating about the clamorous alarm at 1270 Desert Lane *(fictitious address)* and is describing all of Earth Robert's stupidity in having a credit-card doorlock that any little kid could open. Recording all of those things humorously for the kids—they really enjoy them. So you see, you report on all of those things humorously, and others really enjoy reading about them.

And in a recent letter, Ghost Roger spoke about meeting some ghost dogs, who long ago when they were earth dogs lived in a mining camp in the Sierra Nevadas. The dogs talked about the celebration in a mining camp when a baby boy was born. I was that boy.

My grandchildren know about the first spanking I ever got. I was still creeping and my mother took me to Earth Cameron Cabin, down in the valley. I saw Earth Mrs. Cameron put something into a hole. It was charming, bright, and fascinating. So I crept over to some paper in the fireplace and Mrs. Cameron began to spank me. I crawled under the chair where my mother was sitting. She was very resentful. I can still recall that: That great big woman from under the chair, and the peculiar bright dancing thing called fire.

Z: Your memory is extraordinary.

E: I was reading in college about memory. I got a memory and I wrote it out. I checked it out with my mother, and I checked it with my father separately—there are certain falsifications in the memory. I was standing up at the time, holding onto the crib, but I had no crib. I had to be lying down. I am being shown a Christmas tree and there were two things that I really didn't understand that looked alike. They were cats. And there was a man with a lot of hair on his face.

What Christmas was that? My father and mother finally figured it out. My father got so tired of a baby waking up and grabbing him by the whiskers and pulling himself up by them that in February, 1904, he shaved off his beard. It was Christmas, 1903. It took my parents a long time to figure out the time when they took the buckboard and took some cats down to the Cameron Cabin. I squalled furiously. They couldn't understand me and I couldn't understand their stupidity. I wanted to ride beside that sack full of cats. I was two years old. And, of course, we moved to Wisconsin when I was three years old.

The neighbors felt very sorry for me. I had a sister two years younger than me who began talking at the age of one. And the neighbors commiserated with my mother because I was "mentally retarded," because I didn't learn to talk until I was four years old. My mother's answer to the neighbors was, "The boy's too busy." Now Ghost Roger is writing all this.

I think my mother was 28 when my father had a mine in Nevada. My father, who was foreman of the mine, sent for her. She brought my older sister with her to Nevada. Mother was reared by her mother with this understanding: "Never go more than 10 miles away from your home, because if you do you'll die." My grandmother was speaking from her knowledge. My mother went all the way to Nevada.

When she arrived, she was to run the boarding house for the miners. Supplies came in every six months by 20-mule team. Now, how much salt do you order—how much baking soda, how much pepper, how much flour, how much salt pork—how much of everything do you order to run a boarding house for some 20, 30 miners. And at 28 my mother had to figure it out. So I've got the story of Earth Clara and Earth Albert. I write things like that.

Z: *(looking at a picture above the file cabinet behind Erickson's desk)* Are those your parents?

E: Uh-huh. It's a picture of their 65th wedding anniversary.

A professor of psychiatry from South America came to me for psychotherapy. *(This case is reported and discussed in Rosen, 1982a, p. 66, and in Erickson & Rossi, 1977, p. 43.)* I knew him by name and reputation. He was much more brilliant than I—much better educated, much better read. And one of the most arrogant men in the world—very proud of his Castillian blood. Arrogant and proud. He wanted psychotherapy. He talked a foundation into financing his therapy with me. I wondered how on earth would I handle this man—arrogant, proud, much brighter than I, much better educated, much better read. How would you?

Z: I don't know.

E: I knew I'd devise some way. I left it to my unconscious mind. I know my unconscious mind is smarter than I am. So he came in, introduced himself. I took down his name, his age—all the facts. And then I said, "Let's discuss your problem." We had a 2 o'clock appointment. The first interview was two hours long. I asked him his problem. I took a look up at the clock. It was 4 o'clock. And the chair was empty. I opened the manila folder. I could see I had a lot of notes in there. I had lapsed into a trance. Fourteen sessions later, he leapt to his feet and said, "Dr. Erickson, you're in a trance." That awakened me.

Z: *(laughs)*

E: I said, "Yes, I'm in a trance. I knew you were more intelligent than I, better read, and better educated. And knowing how arrogant you are, I made use of my unconscious to do therapy for you. Because nobody's going to outwit my unconscious." He didn't take that with very good grace. Thereafter I continued the interviews in the conscious state.

One day he looked at my parents' picture and said, "Is that your parents?" I said, "Yes." He said, "Your father's occupation?" I said, "A farmer, retired." He said disgustedly, "Oh, peasants." I said, "That's right—peasants. And for all I know, the Viking blood of the bastards of my ancestors may run in your veins."

Z: *(laughs)*

E: And he knew his history. He knew all about the Vikings, raiding, looting, and pillaging all the coasts of Europe—England, Scotland, Wales, Ireland, the Mediterranean. He never again got sarcastic with me.

Z: Uh-huh.

E: The bastards of my Viking ancestors. *(laughs)* He knew and I knew.

One should learn to rely on his unconscious mind in any situation. Most people rely on their conscious mind and they only have available that which their conscious mind can seize upon readily. When you rely on your unconscious mind, you've got a vast store of learnings.

Z: I don't quite understand how to do that or what that really means.

E: Well, "Your parents were peasants," is an insult.

Z: And you responded to that consciously.

E: My unconscious thrust up an answer, based upon past reading.

I'll give you another example. Dr. L. came to Detroit when I was in Michigan. He took a job with the Recorder's Court.

One of the first things he did was go to the Department of Psychology at Wayne State University and point out that he had a Ph.D. as well as an M.D. The chair of the department was getting on in years, and he said they really ought to retire him and take Dr. L. as the head of the department.

Then he went to the Medical School and pointed out to the Dean that he had a Ph.D. as well as an M.D., as well as psychiatric experience. The Dean ought to drop me [*Erickson*] from the faculty, and he would kindly fill my place.

He went to the office of various psychiatrists in Detroit and complained to patients in the waiting room they really ought to see a good psychiatrist [*namely, him*].

When he first arrived in his office, he looked over the woman who was to be his secretary and said, "Miss X, you're rather plain. You're in your mid-30s, never been married. You're prematurely grey. You're cross-eyed, and you're a little overweight. But I wouldn't mind having you for a mistress for awhile." That was Dr. L. She was so infuriated she quit.

Then World War II broke out. He wrote a 17-page, typewritten letter to the Army explaining why he should be commissioned as a general to take care of the mental health of other generals. The Army wrote back, "At the present time, we have no use for a man of your talents." (*Erickson laughs*)

Of course, Dr. L. was not popular in his office. An underling took a carbon copy of Dr. L's original letter and the Army's reply and sent it to a Hearst newspaper which Dr. L. had already antagonized. The paper came out, "Army says it has no use for Dr. L."

Now his secretary had become my secretary. When the paper hit the streets, my secretary read the headline and said, "Let's call on Little Dr. L. [*he was obese*] and weep crocodile tears." I said, "You can call him up if you want to, because when I hit him, it's going to be a mortal wound. I don't know when or how, but I'll let my unconscious work on it. And Little Dr. L. will really know he's been hit.

Now, this was in late July or early August, I don't know which. In November I went to a medical meeting. I was in a side room drinking punch with a lot of other doctors, conversing before the meeting. Little Dr. L. walked in and said, "Hi, Milt—what do you know?" And I said, "All I know is what I read in the newspapers"— Will Rogers' famous remark.

Z: Uh-huh.

E: You couldn't imagine a better reply. You could hear the glasses drop on the table. The other doctors rushed for the telephone; the Hearst newspaper came out with a story: "Erickson tells Dr. L. all he knows is what he reads in the newspaper." And Dr. L. moved to Florida.

I couldn't have consciously figured out any reply as cutting as that. And he furnished the opening. My unconscious was working and it was ready to use anything. There's a lot of things in my unconscious I don't even know about. That's the way the unconscious works. I suddenly remembered Will Rogers' famous remark, and that really hurt Dr. L. in Michigan.

Now, teaching John that I am human has been a slow process. Here and there I say some little thing: I named Mrs. Erickson the "Lady of the House." I'm "The Old Codger." And Barney writes letters about his battles with the Old Codger. And Muffin Woo-Woo in Puerto Rico writes Barney about the Old Codger. Fritz and Jenny write about the Old Codger.

*(Erickson softens his voice)* Now, realize that you have an unconscious mind and you don't have to worry about something. And rely upon your unconscious mind to furnish the right answer—the right movement, at the right time.

I taught the Army Rifle Team about marksmanship. *(An abridged version of this case is reported in Rosen, 1982a, p. 107.)* I didn't have much personal experience. I only had to fire a rifle twice when I was a kid on the farm. The rifle team marksmanship coach read about me and stopped in Phoenix while on a tour. He introduced me to the team and wanted to know if I could use hypnosis because in a marksman's contest, one problem is tension. You fire 40 rounds, you hit a bullseye the first time. Then you think, "Will I hit the third, the fourth, the fifth, the sixth, the seventh?" When you get up to the 30th, your tension is pretty high. He took that problem up with me.

I said, "Yes, I can train the team." I called in a hypnotic subject and did a demonstration; the team agreed I knew my stuff. I went to Fort Benning, Georgia, but the Army wasn't certain I knew my stuff. They threw in two men who had been trying for two years to make the team. Let's say on the basis of a score of 100, they could only make 40, and the lowest passing score was 60. So they threw in those two 40s to train.

I trained the team. They went to an international shoot in Moscow and beat the Russians for the first time. And the two "failures" the Army threw in placed. Because what I taught them was: "First you get the soles of your feet comfortable, your ankles comfortable, your knees comfortable, your thighs comfortable, your hips, torso, your arms, shoulders. Then you get this arm feeling comfortable against the stock of the barrel; then the butt resting very comfortably on your shoulder. Then you enjoy the feeling of your cheek against the stock. And you can move the barrel comfortably back and forth, up and down, over the target. When everything feels perfectly comfortable, you gently squeeze the trigger. That's the way I trained them. I gave them room to modify that in their own way.

One of them who eventually became the National Rifle Champion made a personal modification. The last thing he did was to fit his teeth together. When his teeth felt just right, he squeezed the trigger. (*Erickson laughs*). His nickname is Blinky.

Blinky dropped in a few months ago. After he left the Army team, he tried for the National Rifle Championship. While he was on the Army team, he talked with me about his future. I pointed out that marksmanship skills are necessarily limited by age, and he really ought to live another 50 years. The Winchester Rifle Company hired him to promote the sale of Winchesters. I said, "There's no future in that. There's another champion coming along." I thought he ought to have an occupation that would be meaningful to him. He's a veterinarian now. He dropped in to see me. He was in Phoenix at a veterinarian meeting.

He's been on the Town Council; he's been the Mayor, an Alderman—I don't know what all—in his home city. He's a most popular man there. He has that kind of a personality. He dropped in and reminisced about the Army days—championship days—and his experience in the veterinary business. Things turned out the way I expected them to.

There's another rifle team member who's probably going to be an officer of the American Society of Clinical Hypnosis.

Because when you know you've got a subconscious, you rely on it. One of my lawyer patients came to me and said, "Tomorrow morning. I've got to go to Tucson and take the bar examination. I've failed it five times. I come from Wisconsin. I don't like living there; neither does my wife. We want to move to Arizona and start a family." He said, "Now, can you hypnotize me and get me through the bar examination?"

*(The telephone rings and Erickson answers it. The call is long distance.) (to the man on the telephone)* I've been in a wheelchair since 1965. I haven't got much strength. Your boy would require a great deal of effort, and I'm not up to it physically. *(Erickson hangs up the phone)*

*(to Zeig)* That was a man in New York who has a 16-year-old son on drugs and liquor since the age of 12. The mother has disowned the boy; the father and mother have fought for years. The father finally divorced the mother recently. The boy's a tragedy. There's no hope for him. Now the father's trying to help the boy. He's taken his son to a lot of psychiatrists—Freudian, Jungian, Reichian—trying to straighten the kid out.

I don't like theoretical formulations. Because theoretical formulations—what do they amount to? Is there anything more absurd than a European man who grew up and was educated in Europe, coming to the United States, and trying to understand the past of an American.

I can think of that experience I had in Worcester, Massachusetts. A Russian-German trained psychologist who worked in Wundt's laboratory came to Worcester to get acquainted with American psychology. I found him interesting. He had done excellent research. One evening he suggested we drive to San Francisco and have dinner. From Worcester, Massachusetts to San Francisco for dinner that evening. *(Erickson laughs)* What

was his concept of the United States? (*There's a knock at the door.*
*A patient comes in. We resume the session later.*)

E: Where was I?

Z: You started talking about using the unconscious. You were telling
an anecdote about a lawyer who needed to go to Tucson to take
the bar exam.

Because this case is reported in Zeig, 1980a (p. 58), it will only be
summarized here. Erickson's technique was straightforward. He told
the lawyer to enjoy the scenery on the drive to Tucson and "feel happy
that this was the kind of scenery he would have in his future." On
the way back, he was to enjoy the scenery from a reverse point of
view.

At the exam, he would read the questions and none of them would
make sense. Then he would read the first question a second time and
"a little trickle of information" would flow out of his pen. After the
trickle dried up, he would go on to the next question.

Erickson did not immediately find out if his intervention worked.
However, a year later, just before she was due to deliver, a woman
came to see him for hypnotic childbirth. It was the lawyer's wife.
Erickson's therapy for the woman was to hypnotically suggest that the
lower half of her body belonged to the obstetrician, the upper half
was hers. During the labor and delivery, she would wonder about the
sex of the child, the name, what it would be like to nurse, etc.

Years later, after the birth of the third child, the lawyer returned
and saw Erickson for successful hypnotherapy for back pain.

Then Erickson continues:

E: Now, the unconscious is a lot wiser than you know. (*Erickson
changes his inflection*) You get very thirsty on a hot summer day
and you take a drink and you know it's a good drink. You know
it long before the water has reached the bloodstream. If you get
very thirsty on a cold winter's day, you take a good drink. And
you know it's a good drink long before that water's been absorbed. You didn't count the swallows, but there's a lot of difference between the number of swallows in the summer's drink
and in the winter's drink.

When I first came to Arizona, I told Mrs. Erickson not to salt the food at all. Your salt requirement in the hot desert is much higher than in Michigan. We let the kids salt their food. I made a notation of the number of times they shook the salt cellar—so many times in the summer, so many in the winter. Now how do small children know how to satisfy their salt requirements? If the food didn't have enough salt on it, it didn't taste good.

People come to Arizona from Minnesota, Michigan, Wisconsin and other points east. Adults may suffer terribly from the heat because they continue on with their eastern pattern of salting food. You have to increase your salt intake in the desert. I knew that. I had a lot of patients I had to tell, "Go and salt your food a little bit."

The unconscious knows how much salt, how many swallows of water, and the conscious mind doesn't know a damned thing about it.

Z: More swallows in the summer.

E: More fluid. You see, at 110 degrees you perspire freely and it evaporates immediately because of the humidity—it's 11 percent, 10 percent, 8 percent, 13 percent. If you lean against the car seat, you sweat. But you straighten up and in less than a minute your shirt is perfectly dry. That means you had better drink plenty of fluids. You cannot overload the body with fluid without draining off sodium. So you merely increase your salt intake.

And how do you change your breathing when you are sitting quietly, and then clench your fists. You do alter your breathing. What about your blood pressure? A lie detector, so called, tells you how you change your blood pressure and your breathing when somebody is just talking to you. Your unconscious has that knowledge from frequency of experience.

You can sit in a closed car, drive down the highway, and a bee hits the windshield. Your conscious mind may know that it won't hit you in the face, but you're going to blink and jerk back. You can't control it. Your unconscious says, when an object comes toward you and you see it plainly, you duck.

Z: Uh-huh.

E: And your unconscious mind is conditioned in many ways to bodily needs. If you let the body respond, you can use it.

Now, I got a letter yesterday from a woman, a divorcée, who expects to marry an ex-convict, one of my successes. The trouble so far is her children. They can't understand why the man doesn't say "please." He grew up in a home where "please" was an alien word. He had plenty of time in prison and juvenile hall where you didn't hear the word "please." You heard orders, emphatically given. And you jumped. He had plenty of time where he didn't know the word, "please." Now to hear "Pass the butter" means "Pass the butter." It doesn't mean *"Please* pass the butter." "Shut that door!" That's the language he uses to kids, and they can't understand why he can't say the word "please." Mrs. Erickson and I were discussing that problem this morning. I have to see those kids and explain it to them.

I had an older sister and a younger sister who made my childhood unbearable. They would take something that belonged to me and make me say, "Please; pretty please; pretty, pretty please." They would make me say, "Pretty, pretty, pretty, pretty please—please, please, please." I grew to hate that word, "please." And all my kids wondered, "Why doesn't Daddy say 'please'?" I usually notice that I should have said, 'please.' I practically never say 'please.' Otherwise, I'm polite, but mostly I don't say the word 'please' because I was conditioned against that damned word. But, because my tone of voice is polite, it doesn't hurt people too much.

This ex-convict is harsh in his tone of voice, because that's all he's ever known. He came to me for some advice. *(This case is reported with additional elaboration in Zeig, 1980a, p. 216.)* I gave him good advice. He said, "You know, you can shove that." That isn't the way you talk to a person. And after walking home 12 miles at 109-degree temperature in the summer, he came back and asked, "What was that you said to me?" *(Erickson laughs)* So I told him again, "The help I'll give you is—there's a mattress in my backyard and a blanket. There's an overhanging roof that will protect you from any rain. You can come to the back door; we'll give you cold baked beans to live on. There's a faucet in the backyard for your drinking water. You can stay there and think over whether you want to get over being a drunk. If you want me to take your boots so you won't run away, you'll have to beg me."

He spent five days and nights in the backyard. Then he went out and lined up a job. He joined Alcoholics Anonymous and he goes to Alcoholics Anonymous twice a week. He took his girlfriend there. They're planning to get married on Valentine's Day.

Now, in discussing [with my wife] my own lack of saying 'please,' I brought up the question of my son Robert. You've met him, haven't you?

Z: No, Roxie and I went to his house but he wasn't there and I didn't meet him.

E: Robert can sometimes be brusque in his manners with his family. Why? He was the sweetest-mannered of all eight children. Gentle, sweet. He was also a loner. He was run over by a truck at the age of seven. I identified him at Good Samaritan Hospital. I asked, "What's the damage?" The doctors in the Emergency Room said, "Two broken thighs, a fractured pelvis, body bruises, a fractured skull, and a concussion. We haven't checked yet for internal injuries." I asked, "What's the prognosis?" They said, "Well, if he lives 48 hours, he'll have a chance to survive."

I came home and gathered the family together and said, "We all know Robert. When he does things, he does them well. We can all depend on Robert to do things well. He's just had an accident. Both thighs are broken; his pelvis is fractured; he suffered a concussion, there's no internal injuries. If Robert lives through 48 hours, he will have a chance to live. We'll allow him to do things well. So it's truly impolite to cry. There's nothing you can do. Go get to your homework or your chores. It wouldn't be polite to lose sleep because we can do our job and Robert's going to do his job. You can go to bed comfortably. Because Robert *will* do his part."

We all went to bed as if nothing had happened. Robert did have a hell of a time. He had to put forth an awful lot of effort. When he came home from the hospital, he was awfully excited. He was in a body cast, and the stretcher-bearer brought him in to lie on the couch. And the stretcher-man nearly dropped the stretcher because of what Robert said. Robert said, "I'm so glad I've got parents like you. All the other poor kids saw their parents come every afternoon, and it made the kids cry. Then they came in the evening and made them cry. On Sundays it was awful; the kids were crying all day long. And never once did you come to see me." I said, "No, we wanted you to get well. Actually, we did call the hospital and went to the nurses station and looked through the glass there to see you, but you couldn't see us. And we had the nurses deliver the presents we sent to you."

During my internship on visiting day I took the pulse, blood pressure and respiratory rate of patients before, during and after visitors. Visitors can inadvertently wreck the recovery of a lot of their sick relatives.

Z: So not doing is sometimes the most important. . . .

E: (*overlapping*) The most important thing in the world. When Betty and I were in Chicago, Kristi was staying with friends. She rode a burro. She was 10 years old. The burro walked under an orange tree and knocked her off onto the ground. She broke her elbow. Her friends rushed her to the family doctor who started sweating blood because he was seeing a doctor's child. There was a fracture through the joint. It was a bad fracture. It was a lot of work getting it set properly and getting the cast put on. When it was finally properly set, the doctor made his big mistake. He patted Kristi on the shoulder and said, "Don't worry little girl, you'll get well." She said, "Of course I will! It's a good elbow!" That's the attitude a kid should have.

Now Robert was really put to test. He had to put forth a tremendous effort, and it comes out sometimes in his adjustment to his family. His wife, Kathy, is pregnant now, and he's the most concerned person in the world. He goes out of his way; there's an intensity there.

When he had the cast taken off, he was on the couch. You can't imagine what it is like to come out of a cast after you've been in one from December to March. He turned to the side, looked at the floor and said, "Daddy, do you know that it's as far to the floor as it is to the ceiling?" You get your space disoriented from lying on your back so many months, just seeing the distance from the bed to the ceiling. When he looked to the floor, it seemed just as far away. When he finally mustered courage, he got up to walk out into the kitchen. When you haven't walked for months, you've lost a lot of physical memories, so I walked across the room with him. I knew what was going to happen. The first thing that happens is you forget that you bend at the hips. He bent double and fell to the floor, hard. I said, "I don't think you did too much damage to the floor, Robert. I think the floor can take it all right."

I wondered when he would dare to walk down the front steps. Walking down the front steps was a horrible job, a frightening thing—like trying to jump down the Grand Canyon. So he went out on the porch, and sat up on the railing. He looked at the ground below and he looked at the porch floor. I said nothing. It was he who had to walk down those steps.

One day he walked down the steps and got on his tricycle, and went for a ride. Now, the accident occurred on the corner of Cypress and Third Avenue. I wondered just when he would cross that street, and what I should do about it. He pedaled down to Third Avenue, looked up and down the street, sizing up traffic, looked across the street, sized up the traffic on both sides, and came back. It was a most terrible thing for him, but he did it.

There was one thing more he didn't know about that I didn't know about. His mother took him to the dentist. The dentist was on the second floor. The stairway was made of slats; you could look through the slats and see the ground below. He started up the stairs and said, "Go ahead. I'll meet you at the dentist's office." He went up all by himself. I can assure you it must have been a very frightening experience. He came out of the dentist's office and said, "Mama, you go get the car. I will meet you at such and such a street corner." He walked down the stairway by himself, forcing himself to walk normally. Do you have any idea what a horrible experience and what kind of self-control was required for that?

When I was a little kid on the farm a man hanged himself in the woods a mile and a half away. All the neighboring farmers said his ghost was there. They would drive three miles out of their way rather than drive the highway through that woods; they would drive around it.

Now I'd been badly frightened by my playmates who told me, "If you dream the same dream three times in succession, it will come true." I dreamed about a tiger trying to get me three nights in a row. I was really afraid that the tiger would come out of the dark. When I learned about that ghost, I waited for a dark, stormy night with the moon out. I walked slowly a mile and a half through the woods. Then I turned around and walked slowly back, rustling up the leaves, flicking the limbs of the trees. Small animals were rustling away—the skunks, the mice, and so on. I knew what a struggle was. After that, I never had much of a sense of fear at all.

Z: Saying there are some things you have to do for yourself.

E: *(overlapping)* . . . for yourself. But it leaves a conditioned pattern of behavior behind you with a great intensity.

When I work with a patient, I'm decidedly intense. It's important for the patient. In my medical school, psychiatry had been taught by a surgeon. In a desultory fashion he narrated his experiences in surgery. He gave an examination by bringing a couple of bottles of whiskey and glasses and saying, "Here's the exam, boys."

When I joined the medical faculty in Michigan, in my first lecture I said, "All of you students know every college professor thinks that his course is the most important course, which is ridiculous. I'm not that kind of a professor. I don't think my course is the important course; I *know* it is." (*Zeig and Erickson laugh*)

I really shocked them when I said, "I *know* it is." Then I gave them a reading list. And then for those really interested in psychiatry, there was a secondary list. After the first class many students signed a petition asking the Dean to drop me from the faculty. The Dean told me about it. I said, "I don't like it one bit. I'm serious about teaching." The Dean said, "What do you want me to do with this?" Erickson said, "Give it to me. I'll take care of it." About six weeks later, by which time the students really liked me and liked the course, I put the petition on the blackboard when they came in one morning. I never said a word about it. Nobody asked anything about it. What could they do? *(Erickson laughs)*

The Senior Class always gave a skit at their graduation celebration. There were four professors that were selected. There was one they all disliked intensely. There was a skit one year, and they placed an old chamber pot on the table. They all filed past and said, "Good Morning, Doctor X." *(Erickson laughs)*

Now there was Dr. Rachel. Rachel was the internist, and he had an unusual ability. Six students could crowd around him and simultaneously ask him a question, and he would reply to all six questions. He separately heard all six simultaneous questions. Of course, he was included in that skit. The questions put to the man who was imitating him were very complex and long. And he would recite the correct answers to those elaborate questions, one after another.

Then there was Pete Jaspers. Here's an example of Pete Jaspers. I was at the induction board. I examined a selectee and put a red "R" on his forms, rejecting him. The selectee was a fine-looking young man, well developed and muscular. As he walked past Jaspers' booth, Jaspers looked at him and saw that red "R." He said, "What goddamned fool rejected a man like this? Sit down." The selectee sat down. Jaspers examined him very carefully and put down a second red "R." He wandered over to my booth and said, "You know, I'm the same kind of a goddamned fool." *(Erickson laughs)*

He was conducting a class in neurology for my residents, and he asked Joe, a very bright chap, "What's the proper treatment for—" and then he named an obscure neurological disease. Joe gave the prescription correctly. And Jaspers said, "You pointed-headed idiot, what goddamned fool did you get that misinformation from?" Joe said, "I read an article." He named the paper, published by Dr. Peter Jaspers. Jaspers said, "I've *learned* something since then." *(Erickson laughs)* A perfect answer. He was always included in the skits.

And they also included me. I had a great big purple bow tie, a couple of manuscripts in my hand, making that famous statement, "I've got a minor reading list for the class." Then they unrolled a manuscript about 20 feet long. "And for those who are slightly interested in psychiatry. . . ." And then there was a second roll. "And for those most definitely interested in psychiatry. . . ." And then there was a third roll. (*Erickson laughs*) There were 40 books in the first list, 20 on the second, about 50 on the third.

Next Erickson tells the story of Anne (reported in Rosen, 1982a, p. 231). She was a top medical student who was chronically late. People at the medical school wondered how Erickson would deal with that. On the first day of her enrollment in Erickson's class, he salaamed to her when she came in late. The faculty, students, and staff spent that day salaaming to Anne. After that she was punctual.

Erickson merely "paid tribute," yet the intervention changed Anne's pattern when others had failed.

Z: I'd like to ask a question. You have an extraordinary ability to attend to minimal cues in the words and movements of other people. I would like to develop some of those skills for myself. Do you have some suggestions?

E: Whenever you make an observation, record it on paper and date it. Lock it away. When you have positive proof or negative proof, go back and read your original observation. If you say, "I think that girl is having an affair," write it down. It may be three months before you get proof that she's having an affair. You can't remember if you wrote down, "She's having a love affair." You may have written down, "I think she fancies so and so." Or, "I think she's falling in love." You don't remember what you wrote three months ago, so you go back to that locked drawer and you look up that original observation you wrote down. That way you learn which ones were correct.

Z: Uh-huh.

E: And you will learn an awful lot. Months later you discover something and you say, "Oh, yeah, I noticed that months ago." However, you might not have. Maybe you did; maybe you didn't. Maybe you thought of something else. Because you can't even remember what your understandings were last week. But when you record them and use them, you check up on your ability.

Here Erickson tells a case (reported in Rosen, 1982a, p. 182) in which he diagnosed a transvestite patient by noticing that when she brushed lint off her sleeve, she didn't "detour her elbow" in the fashion that women commonly do.

E: By the time my daughters got to be 11 or 12, I knew what size breasts they would have when they grew up. Because the human body makes provisions for coming events, and it makes thorough provisions. Within two weeks after conception, there is a massive change in the calcium of the skeletal bones. That conception is almost microscopic in size; however, the body knows what's going on.

Now one of my preteen daughters happened to reach out to pick up something on the radio. I noticed her elbow detour. So I asked Mrs. Erickson to watch our daughter when she took a bath, and to look in and see if there was any change in my daughter's nipples. Betty told me, "There's just the beginning of unfolding of the nipples."

I thought I should tell her that she was going to have midget breasts. It was only a small detour. I pointed out to her that midget breasts were very satisfactory. When you grow older, they wouldn't hang down in your lap. You never had to throw them over your shoulder to wash under them.

And then one day I told her that I owed her an apology. If she ever got married and nursed a baby, she'd have medium-large breasts, and then they would shrink back to midget size after she weaned the baby. She had been baby-sitting a nursing infant and I'd seen a wider detour of her elbow. Now she's nursed her own babies. She's got midget-sized breasts, and I knew that when she was 10 years old. And when she was 12, I knew that she would have medium-large breasts if she got pregnant, and they would shrink. And she now believes me whenever I tell her anything about anatomy or physiology.

Z: I'll bet.

E: How many people watch people walk? Move their arms, their
   hands, their elbows?

   Now there was a great line of inductees at the selection board.
They were all crowding up around the booths which made the
psychiatric examination difficult. No selectee wanted to have
someone eavesdrop, so I said, "OK boys, form a line." One of
them dispiritedly went to the end of the line. I told him, "Bus
driver, come in." And that chap came in. He said, "How did
you know I was a bus driver?" I said, "How long have you been
yelling, 'Move to the rear. Move to the rear. Move to the rear.' "
*(Erickson laughs)* He said, "I've been yelling it so long and nobody
does it. When you said, 'Get in line. Move back,' I wanted people
to move back desperately." *(Erickson laughs)* It's just common
sense.

   I worked my way through medical school doing psychological
examinations for the institutionalized inmates of the correctional
and penal institutions of Wisconsin, including inmates at the
Milwaukee County House of Correction. I know a lot about
crime. I was a consultant for the courts in Detroit for 14 years.
That's how I knew how to tell Pete, "You want help. You're a
drunk. You're an ex-con. You've been working for drinks;
sponging off your girlfriend for food and lodging. She got sick
of it and threw you out. Now you want help. There's a mattress
in my backyard. Stay there as long as necessary. I'll furnish you
a blanket. There's a faucet in the backyard, and you can have
cold, baked beans if you come to the back door." "You know
where you can shove that," he said and walked out. He walked
miles in the hot sun to his girlfriend who said, "Get out of here.
I'm sick and tired of you." So he came back to me.

   I had a man walk into my office in Michigan. *(Compare this
rendering of this case with the celebrated version reported in Wilk,
1985, p. 216.)* He said, "I'm 42 years old. I hold many records
in aviation. I began drinking at the age of 12. I'm just off a three-
month-long binge." I asked, "What did you do before that?"
"Well, I had just sobered up from another three-month binge.
I've come to you because you're Scandinavian. So am I. And one
squarehead can talk straight from the shoulder to another squarehead. Squareheads can take it from squareheads."

*(to Zeig)* You know that term, don't you—squarehead? "Erickson" is Scandinavian. A Scandinavian is a "Squarehead."

I said, "All right. So you've been an alcoholic for 30 years. You hold several aviation records." He said, "Yes, I'm the 22nd member of the Caterpillar Club."

*(to Zeig)* Do you know what that is? That's when you're in a plane and you tell your Engineer to bail out. When he safely bails out, you bail out. And if you live, you become a member of the Caterpillar Club. It was in the early days, in his teens.

He said, "I have a scrapbook of the stories of my aviation records." I looked through it. He was a friend of General "Hap" Arnold in the U.S. Air Force in World War II. He flew the same time Hap Arnold had. He had made an early transcontinental flight. I don't know how many contests he had won. And now he was sponging on his parents, just coming off a three-month binge, preceded by a three-month binge.

I said, "All right. In the first place, that's not your scrapbook. You're just a plain drunk. You're a parasite on good people, on good parents and a good wife. You're a bum. You beg, you sneak, and you claim to be the owner of that scrapbook. The man who set those records was a man, and you definitely are not a man." And for a couple of hours, I gave him a choice review of what he was.

I asked him how he usually got drunk, because drunks have a pattern. He said, "I order two schooners of beer, one for each hand. I empty the schooners into my mouth and then I follow with a chaser of whiskey." Erickson said, "When you leave here, if you're man enough, go down to your car. Drive down Livernois Avenue. Stop at Middle Belt. Go into Millstadt Tavern. Order two schooners of beer." He was furious. What I said was awfully unpleasant. He left the office and he banged down the stairs.

He later told me that he stopped at the tavern, and ordered and had two schooners of beer in his hand. He suddenly realized, "I am doing exactly what that son-of-a-bitch said I would do." He said, "So I put 'em down, and I haven't had a drink since then. I didn't even have those drinks. I paid for them and just walked out." I replied, "And you're wearing a halo for that?

You've been cheating thoroughly! You've been on 'goof balls' all week." He said, "How did you know?" I said, "I know alcoholics." So then I really told him what he was. And he knew I was right. That was on September 26, 1942.

That same day, he went to downtown Detroit and signed up at a gymnasium. He worked out every day, getting himself into good physical shape. In November he was taken back into the Air Force but not given flying status. He was a Captain, but he was grounded. He was a good military man. He would call me up from the air base and say, "I'm weakening." Once he called me and said, "I've got a bottle of rum here, what do I do with it?" I said, "Bring it over to my apartment. I'll furnish the glasses and ice. We'll get drunk together." He came over. I had two glasses with ice in them. I filled my glass, and I filled his. I started drinking. He said, "You God damned lousy son-of-a-bitch! You would get drunk with me!" I said, "Isn't that what the bottle of rum is for?" He said, "God damn you!" and walked out.

Another time, he came over and said, "You told me any time I wanted to go on a drunk, you'd go with me. So I've got my car here." I said, "Fine." I called Betty and told her not to expect me and not to worry. I said, "Which bar?" He told me. I said, "Fine." It was in East Dearborn. I rode in the car comfortably two miles, three miles, four miles. We were just chatting about casual things.

Finally, he said, "You son-of-a-bitch, you meant it when you said you would go with me to a bar and get drunk." I said, "Yes. I think I can drink you under the table. Anyway we'll find out." He said, "God damn you. Damn you. Damn you. You're not going to find out." He turned the car around and went back home.

He was elevated to the status of Major. He came in one evening. He greeted me, "Good evening." And I said, "Good evening, Major." He said, "I lose that bet. I had bet you wouldn't notice it immediately."

He used to take us out to the officers' mess downtown. He always ordered a nice drink for Betty and a nice drink for me.

He ordered orange juice or milk for himself. He got his flying status back and was sent to the Pentagon where he became a special pilot for Pentagon officials and Congressmen.

Now and then he called me from Washington saying, "I think I need to hear your voice." And we would chat about various things. It might be a week later, it might be three weeks later before he called me again. September 26, 1942 was his last drink. He came to see us, I guess in 1963, with his wife and child. He took us out to dinner, ordered a drink for Betty and me. He still hasn't had a drink.

He came in saying, "I'm a squarehead like you are." He wanted me to talk straight from the shoulder. I can talk straight from the shoulder. I promised him I would get drunk with him anytime he wanted to get drunk. When he took me up on that, he chickened out. All the way back home, I laughed at him for chickening out. I didn't praise him; I ridiculed him for chickening out.

Once when Hap Arnold came back from Europe, he and Hap Arnold and some high officials (he was a Lieutenant-Colonel then) were having a visit in the officers' mess. Bob got called to the phone. In his absence, Hap Arnold spiked his Coca-Cola. Bob came back and had a swallow of that Coca-Cola before he realized it had been spiked. Even though he was in uniform and Hap Arnold was a general, he turned to Hap Arnold and said, "You lousy son-of-a-bitch," and he really let out a blast. And Hap Arnold realized he had done something absolutely unforgivable. You don't spike a reformed alcoholic's drink. Hap Arnold took the blistering he got and apologized. And you don't swear at Generals. *(Erickson laughs)* But Hap Arnold was a good man and unafraid to face the truth. You can do anything to an inferior in the Army except violate absolute rights. Even General Patton found out you can't slap a Private and that you apologize to a Private. Spiking a drink for a reformed alcoholic is perhaps worse than slapping a Private. It's an unforgivable thing. And after he got through with Hap Arnold, he went and got hydrogen peroxide and used it for mouthwash. Then he brushed his teeth. It was horrible.

He had one bad experience when he left Detroit for the Pentagon. His squadron gave him a farewell banquet in which they served rum-flavored cake. He took one bite and recognized the rum flavor, and got nauseated. He told me later, "I had a hell of a time brushing my teeth and gargling to get that taste out of my mouth."

Had I tried a relatively orthodox way of treating an alcoholic, where would I have been? You meet patients at their level. You use the language they understand, and you're not afraid to use it.

Often you find patients who would like certain kinds of language. But they can't bear to say it themselves. So you say it for them. I can think of a state hospital patient who vomited up everything. She always vomited. The superintendent said, "She's going to starve to death in spite of tube feeding. Can you do something?" I said, "The sky's the limit?" He said, "The sky's the limit."

I went and told the woman I was going to tube feed her and if necessary I would give her a second tube feeding. My intention was that the first tube feeding would teach her to keep it in her stomach. I put her in a chair and restrained her. She was perfectly comfortable about that. Her hands were fastened to the arms of the chair, and the nurse had a dish pan for her to vomit into. I poured the tube feeding down. She vomited it up. I poured it from the dishpan back into the tube. She threw part of it up. I poured it back. She learned to keep it down.

Z: I'll bet.

E: The nurses got so damned sick of me; they really wanted to have me fired. I preferred their wrath to the dying of the patient. I used a simple measure.

The last case Erickson discussed this day is the case of Herbert, a hospitalized schizophrenic, on whom Erickson used strategic tasks to confront and get Herbert to break through his delusions. Because it is reported in detail in Haley (1973, p. 287) and Rosen (1982a, p. 202) it is not reprinted here.

## Comment

I would like to share some of my reactions to reading the transcript of my sessions with Erickson. They were personal reactions that were moving, and professional reactions that were every bit as intriguing as they were when I first met Erickson 12 years ago. I will first describe some of the subjective ones.

My overt reason for coming to Erickson was to be a student; other reasons for my visit were not concretely clarified in my mind. However, although it was unstated, Erickson was clearly working to influence me on a personal level. I didn't present or request help with my problems—some problems I didn't even perceive. Erickson picked up on my areas of personal difficulty and proceeded to help me surmount them. I was pleased that he was trying to help me overcome blocks that would limit me as a person and a practitioner.

I vividly remember how emotionally touched I was by the experience of being with Erickson. On the second day of my visit I watched him struggle to move himself from his wheelchair to his office chair. Then he started speaking to me through his obvious pain, intent on instructing me about how to be more effective as a person and therapist. I remember feeling powerfully moved that he would selflessly spend his limited energy to help me.

No powerful figure I had met before had such a moving impact. There was something extraordinary about Erickson: Perhaps his profound effect was due to his acute sensitivity, respect for the individual, intensity, verve, uniqueness, and joie de vivre in the face of adversity. I saw him struggle to bring out the best in himself and it inspired me to want to do the same.

During the sessions, I tried to extract patterns and consciously comment on Erickson's method. However, I sometimes disrupted his process. He had his goals in mind and worked without needing much conversation from me. I was surprised (and even a bit relieved) by his technique of being active; little was required from me. However, I was not merely passive; throughout the sessions I was challenged to process what Erickson was doing and it was my efforts that would energize the changes.

As a more experienced therapist now and aided by additional years of study of Erickson's methods, I scrutinized his techniques more closely on a professional level. One particular technique stood out: Some of Erickson's anecdotes lulled me. Then it seemed that Erickson would "slip in" suggestions when I was in a more responsive state. This technique of "intentional irrelevance" to lull the conscious mind deserves closer study.

Also, Erickson tried to help me improve my ability to learn hypnosis both personally and professionally. In his inductions with me he used only naturalistic techniques. There were no formal inductions of hypnosis; none were requested. In fact, at that time I probably would have been scared and resistant of formal hypnosis. It seemed that Erickson used the right technique and thereby enhanced my responsiveness.

This transcript shows Erickson as he was as a teacher and a therapist. Because the entire transcript is presented, Erickson's process can be studied. Oftentimes writers analyze Erickson's moment-to-moment interventions; however, his effectiveness was rooted in his use of ongoing process. But, developing insight into the process of Ericksonian therapy is beyond the scope of this volume.

# Appendix A

---

**My Life Story**

by

Diane Chow

Owing to a bit of carelessness on my mother's part I was born. I was a twin and when my father saw that there were two of us, he offered to drown one, but my mother felt very important. I often wondered why being a twin made me welcome when one baby wasn't wanted.

My father bought my mother a diamond lavalier and a grand piano to celebrate. Nobody ever learned to play the piano, but the bench came in handy, as it was just the right height for me to cut my second year molars on. My brother stole the diamond lavalier along with everybody's war savings stamps and dime banks.

We weren't poor. My mother told me that people used to stand by our house and curse because we had so much coal we couldn't get it in the basement. Other people were freezing. This must have made my mother feel important, too—if people had asked her for coal, she would have given it to them if they showed the proper amount of gratitude.

My mother was very pretty. My earliest memory of her is reaching out to touch her dress when she and dad went to the country club dance.

My father was tall and slim and humorous, but the only responsibility he felt toward us children was that of providing us with enough money to keep us happy. I don't know what kind of an alcoholic you'd call dad. He'd work industriously for six months and meekly submit to my mother's bossing and then suddenly he'd. . . .*

You suggested the hospital. I didn't want to—yet I knew I would. I thought back—the Receiving Ward—snotty attendants—afraid to leave again—tired—ashamed to complain of physical ailments that worried me—because even when I had appendicitis in the hospital, they laughed and told me it was "all in my head"—everything in Pontiac is "all in your head."

You know the rest. I wished I had courage to die first, and then I could see your face and I bawled myself out. I thought that you must believe I could get well, or you wouldn't give me your time. I got in before I could change my mind. I want to get well. I'm just afraid I'll fail you. I'm not very brave. I know that, underneath, my mind isn't a nice thing at all. I'll probably do anything to keep you from knowing it.

That's all. I've written this fast, just as it came to me. It isn't a masterpiece and the writing is poor. However, it gave me a sore arm, a stiff neck and my head is very tired.

I can't finish the story of my life as I'm not dead yet and I'm not even sure I want to die anymore—but—oh, how I hate to get up in the morning!

---

*Thus ends the first page of Diane's autobiography. The next section is page 37 of her typed life story.

# Appendix B

## Eva Parton

The patient made the statement, "You just ask me questions and I'll answer them." She was asked how old she was. "Don't tell me you don't know that. I'm thirty-two years old, or I'm supposed to be thirty-two years old. I was born July 16, 1912, in Herclian, Missouri. It's a small town—small-town gossip—over the back fence like dishwater—like dishwater slop that you throw out to the pigs. Two-legged sluts and snakes in the form of human beings. There are a lot of people I don't like. One of them is the lady that raised me. I worshipped the man who raised me. He was white as a lily, and his hair was as black as the raven—as Edgar Allen Poe says—the raven of the night. His eyes were yellow as leopards, but he was one leopard that never changed his spots. He was white, and his mother was dark. He had an older brother who dominated the family, and he put his wife in the insane asylum. She's been there for thirty-four years of her life. She's in another place in Missouri now, where they have padded cells so you don't dash your brains out against the walls. She was released under his care about eighteen years ago, and the dirty lousy son-of-a-bitch got her pregnant. She was placed back in the institution then and her little boy is now eighteen years old. She has been there ever since.

"My sister-in-law, Norma Kowalski, the wife of my half-brother, Jacob Kowalski, who lives at 12345 Braille in Detroit—my half-brother, told me that my aunt remembered everything. When I went to Missouri on the fourth of July with my son, Ralph, who is seven years old—my brother Paul—I think he was the one who made the phone call for the police to come and pick me up at the Greyhound bus station—he said I was ready for the psychopathic ward. When I seen my brother Paul at the ticket window I went down to the ladies' rest room and took Ralph with me. We waited till they called the bus to St. Louis—until they called the last bus to St. Louis. After I had called up my girl friend who lives on Pilgrim in Detroit—her husband does first-class moving in the Indian Village neighborhood—for the best people—she's my best girl friend—we worked together in a hotel in 1932. She's like a sister to me. I was her bridesmaid in 1933.

"I was a waitress and a hostess in the hotel for three or four years. Some days I liked it there and some days I didn't. I quit about three times. When the man looked at me as if I was without any clothes on it used to embarrass me, but I don't get embarrassed as I used to before I was married. I quit the first time over a German waiter. I fell in love with him. I was twenty-one. He was a married man and he took off his wedding ring and I thought he was single. He made a date with me, and my girl friend found out he was married and she told me. I didn't believe it because I didn't think anyone could play a lousy dirty trick like that on a girl who had never been married. So I went to Pam, the cashier, and asked her if he was married. She said yes, she knew that for sure, and his wife was pregnant. I had a date with him for that night so I sent Peter, one of the room-service waiters, up to Hyman on the fifth floor where he was serving dinner, and told him that I wouldn't keep the date. Then I went to Barbara's room that night. She was the cashier on the fifteenth floor. I stayed with her all night and never went to sleep that night. So that's why I quit the first time—over the married German waiter.

"After his baby was born, we did go out together again. I wanted to kiss him to see what it did feel like. I already knew what it felt like when I didn't kiss him, and I wanted to see if it was as good as when I kissed him. It was, and I went out with him quite a number of times, but we never had intercourse. He brought his little girl up to my house when she was nine months old. Her name was Mary. She never did go to strangers, but she stayed with me all morning.

"We went to Belle Isle and took pictures of her. I snapped a picture of Bill, one of the waitresses' boy friends, while I was taking pictures. Then when he had these pictures developed at the J. L. Hudson Company there was Bill's picture with the other ones, and Hyman was very much put out. So he questioned me, and I said, 'You've a lot of right to question me—when you're a married man. That man is Doris Devlin's boy friend, and I took that picture on her day off, so I hope you're completely satisfied.'

"He wanted me to leave and go to Chicago with him, and leave his wife, but I said, no, it might be a funny kind of love but I loved him too much, because I knew some day he would get tired of me and come back to his wife and his little girl, because blood's supposed—*supposed* to be thicker than water. If I had been smart I would have taken the chance and gone to Chicago and lived with him, but I was only twenty-one, and I didn't know a lot of the things about life. I never had talked with my mother because it embarrassed me to talk to my mother. I never undressed in front of my mother, and I could have undressed in front of my father and my brothers and thought nothing of it. I had a funny feeling in front of my mother. One time she took off her clothes in front of me and I left the room.

"During this time I was paroled to Eloise. When my mother said my father had died I simply said, 'You're a goddamned liar. My father will never be dead.' And as I became more well I never felt that my father was dead. What you keep in your heart is your own ideas regardless of what other people think—and no matter what visions they think you see or what voices they think you hear. I'm not so God damn jerky as people think I am. It's the people I live with—like my father used to say, lie down with a bunch of fleas and you'll get up with the fleas. I used to hear him say things like that. My mother used to say eavesdroppers hear no good of themselves. I had a grandmother who used to talk to my father and I used to listen to them. She was black Irish. I'm Irish and I'm Indian and I'm English and I'm Welsh and Indian and German and what else I don't know. As my brother used to always say, 'We're indirectly connected with the Lloyds of London,' but then he always had a line of bull from here to St. Louis. When he was in high school I did all his home work—he never had to study. I had to study certain subjects. I was very good in gym and in music and in English and I liked history and vocational information. I didn't care much about biology—I didn't like to cut up stuff. I never liked to pick butterflies and mount them—we did that in grade school—but my brother Paul liked biology. He liked to torture things—in one way he was like my husband. My husband liked to see people when they were tortured—he liked to watch their reactions. My mother said he was crazy—but he wasn't crazy. He had a brilliant mind like my brother Paul, and my husband and I would be together today if it wasn't for Margret Ross—the dirty bitch. I always say there's decent bitches and there's alley bitches, and a decent bitch is a decent bitch, and an alley bitch is an alley bitch. In the Bible it tells you that a whore is someone who sells her body, but I never sold my body, but I intend to when I get out of this place, because I'm tired of working so damn hard for what I get out of the world and I'm not going to work any more."

# Appendix C

## Millie Parton

First of all, I am not a patient here. I was brought here by my aunt and my uncle, two days ago. I am quite certain my aunt had good intentions. She thought I needed some treatment of some sort—just what I haven't the vaguest notion. They had me in Bellevue in New York City while I was there. I have been living there off and on for the past three years. I might say mostly off, because my husband has been in service all that time so I came home and stayed with my aunt and uncle 'till he was discharged in Chicago. He was in the hospital for twelve weeks there.

I love my aunt and uncle very much. I am sure they have good intentions, as I said. My uncle Walter is of German descent. My mother's name was Bonnie Skate. She was one of three girls. Rae is the youngest and the middle one is June. She had a daughter—no, two daughters, I believe—I'm not sure. She had one daughter, at any rate—June did—Chris. And Rae has no children. I am Bonnie's daughter, and my mother died at the time of my birth. I was born in Palmer Hospital in Detroit, Michigan.

My uncle raised me and he was very good to me. I was happy there until I grew up. Then—well, I think everyone gets to an age where they want to have their own home—there's nothing wrong or unnatural about that, is there? But they were very possessive with me and wouldn't let me be with John for some unknown reason. They had never seen him, at least I didn't think they had even met the boy to my knowledge. But afterwards I found out since I came home that they had. They have tried to keep us separated, and I won't stand for it—do you understand?

I never have been legally adopted. My birth certificate is here in Detroit at the Board of Health, and it said "Baby Parton" on it. I have found out since my name should be Caroline, but I'm going under the name of Millie. Caroline was my middle name—you undertstand? But all during my business associations I have worked under the name of Millie. I have worked ever since I was seventeen, and I have used the name of my foster-father, which is Buntig, which is a German name. Why there should be anything wrong with using a German name, I don't know. But it seems that every time there is a war in this country, people with German names have one hell of a time. And just why that is I should certainly like to know! And I had trouble in New York three years ago when the war started because of my name. So John changed it for me, and it became Mr. and Mrs. John T. Phillips. John is better known to me as Jack—my husband, if you don't mind. He's wonderful. He's in the medical corps. He was, I should say, but he has been reinstated now, I am sure.

He was discharged as an N.P. Of course you know what that means! Why I don't know, because he is not a psychoneurotic nor has he ever been one. The Army apparently kept him in the hospital in Chicago for twelve weeks, or someone did, and I have a faint idea who it was. It was my foster-parents who had something to do with it—or my uncle. Bob Herman, an attorney-at-law in Detroit. He had a lot to do with this thing. He has never liked me even as a child, and Chris has been out in the world, too. I don't know what he has done—not anything that I know of definitely. I mean—you know, you have to have proof before you can accuse people of things. I don't just know—but I'll tell you this: There's something wrong some place!

I asked him for help when I was at Bellevue. I asked the Judge to see my uncle, and the Judge told me I could see my uncle. But I have never seen him yet. And I asked to see Lieutenant Fox of the Army WACs at the Army Recruiting Station where I went and joined, and I have been AWOL since the 28th of September. And the Judge told me I could see Lieutenant Fox, and do you know what happened? They sent me to Bellevue and to Rockland State in Orangeburg, New York. The Judge did that!

I came home, though. My aunt came down and got me and we stayed at a hotel in Brooklyn where I had never been in my life, for two nights, and then we came back to Detroit. And that was about—let me see—what day is today—Friday? We got back—it will be two weeks Sunday. And they have kept me tied in the house practically all that time ever since. I understand why now. They didn't want me to contact John. In fact it came to quite an issue. I mean we had a regular—what should I say—a regular fight about it in the apartment, which was undoubtedly overheard. So they had me brought here. If anyone needs treatment it's my aunt. She is not well, nor has she been since the menopause. She has varicose veins in her left leg, and they swell all the time, and she has had bad trouble for a long time with her back. She has a sway back—you know what I mean—like this? (Here the patient gestured with her hand.) I haven't got that kind of a back. I've got one just as straight as an arrow—just like my grand-mother's. But she does need treatment, but I don't want her to have it in a place like this. Well, maybe the hospital part of it is all right here. I don't know—I've never been here before. But I would prefer that she be taken to Ann Arbor. I have been here for two days. That's all I can tell you.

(At this point it was suggested that the patient tell the incident about the ice-box in the apartment house where she had lived.) Oh, I would like to tell you about that. It was awful. You know how I got to Bellevue in New York. This isn't very long ago. In fact, I went back there on the 23rd of July, 1944, because Jack had been discharged from and Army and he went from Chicago to New York, and I wanted to be with him—naturally. So he lived at the Manhattan Hotel at first. I went right there and I stayed there continuously—outside of spending two weeks at the Madison Hotel. Jack and I lived at that hotel about a week when we were first married. Previous to that we lived on Bank Street in the Village for about three days, but I didn't care for it in the Village so we moved up to Manhattan proper and went to the Madison. Naturally I remembered that hotel and went back to it because it was less expensive. That was on the East Side. I wasn't very keen about it. So I removed myself and went back to the Manhattan again. Then I came back home again because Betty, a girl I met in the Paddock, took my wallet with the only pictures in it that I had of Jack. I'm not certain it was she, but there were only four of us in the part, Betty and myself and two soldiers. One of the soldiers was named Robert Smith. He went AWOL and was with me for a time and we lived together, and he missed his ship. So he was court-martialed and lost his pay—twelve dollars a week, I guess or something like that. You know what they do in the Army. I wasn't at all responsible for his missing his ship. He wanted to go, you understand, but he didn't want to leave me either. Why I haven't the slightest notion. Well, I won't say that, either, because he asked me to marry him and be a good girl until he came back and all that sort of stuff, but after all I was married to John. He wrote to me in the Madison under the name of Smith. He addressed me as his wife, Mrs. R. Smith.

So I went back to the Manhattan and stayed there again because I didn't care about the East Side any more. It seemed like I ran into people I didn't care too much for. It's really nicer on the West Side. That hotel is about three blocks from Central Park, I think—off-hand. Well, in fact I know it is three blocks from the Park—on 57th Street. It's about the widest street in Manhattan proper. Well, then, one day I talked to John on the phone. He used to work in the ship-building yards in Manhattan, and when he had a little time on his lunch hour he would call me up on the phone. So one day he said that I should look for an apartment. He said, "It's kind of expensive there, don't you think, honey?" So I started looking for an apartment. Remember that day of the hurricane? I was looking for an apartment that day—for the Army Air Force Psychiatrist, Lieutenant Reed, who expected his wife and child to arrive the following Sunday. . . .

# References

Bateson, G. & Ruesch, J. (1951). *Communication: The Social Matrix of Psychiatry*. New York: W.W. Norton.

Beahrs, J.O. (1971). The hypnotic psychotherapy of Milton H. Erickson. *American Journal of Clinical Hypnosis, 14*, 73-90.

Berne, E. (1966). *Principles of Group Treatment*. New York: Grove Press.

Corley, J.B. (1982). Ericksonian techniques with general medical problems. In J.K. Zeig (Ed.), *Ericksonian Approaches to Hypnosis and Psychotherapy* (pp. 287-291). New York: Brunner/Mazel.

Dammann, C.A. (1982). Family therapy: Erickson's contribution. In J.K. Zeig (Ed.), *Ericksonian Approaches to Hypnosis and Psychotherapy* (pp. 193-200). New York: Brunner/Mazel.

Erickson, M.H. (1944). The method employed to formulate a complex story for the induction of an experimental neurosis in a hypnotic subject. *Journal of General Psychology, 31*, 191-212.

Erickson, M.H. (1966). The interspersal technique for symptom correction and pain control. *American Journal of Clinical Hypnosis, 3*, 198-209.

Erickson, M.H. (1973). A field investigation by hypnosis of sound loci importance in human behavior. *American Journal of Clinical Hypnosis, 16*, 92-109.

Erickson, M.H., Haley, J., & Weakland, J. (1959). A transcript of a trance induction and commentary. *American Journal of Clinical Hypnosis, 2*, 49-84.

Erickson, M.H. & Rossi, E.L. (1974). Varieties of hypnotic amnesia. *American Journal of Clinical Hypnosis, 4*, 225-239.

Erickson, M.H. & Rossi, E. (1977). The autohypnotic experiences of Milton H. Erickson. *American Journal of Clinical Hypnosis, 20,* 36-54.

Haley, J. (Ed.) (1967). *Advanced Techniques of Hypnosis and Therapy. Selected papers of Milton H. Erickson, M.D.* New York: Grune & Stratton.

Haley, J. (1973). *Uncommon Therapy, The Psychiatric Techniques of Milton H. Erickson, M.D.* New York: W.W. Norton.

Haley, J. (1980). *Leaving Home.* New York: McGraw-Hill.

Haley, J. (1982). The contribution to therapy of Milton H. Erickson, M.D. In J.K. Zeig (Ed.), *Ericksonian Approaches to Hypnosis and Psychotherapy* (pp. 5-25). New York: Brunner/Mazel.

Haley, J. (1984). *Ordeal Therapy.* San Francisco: Jossey-Bass.

Haley, J. & Weakland, J. (1985). Remembering Erickson. In J.K. Zeig (Ed.), *Ericksonian Psychotherapy, Volume I: Structures* (pp. 585-604). New York: Brunner/Mazel.

Hammond, D.C. (1984). Myths about Erickson and Ericksonian hypnosis. *American Journal of Clinical Hypnosis, 26,* 236-245.

Karpman, S.B. (1968). Script drama analysis. *Transactional Analysis Bulletin, 26,* 39-45.

Lankton, C.H. (1985). Generative change: Beyond symptomatic relief. In J.K. Zeig (Ed.), *Ericksonian Psychotherapy, Volume I: Structures* (pp. 137-170). New York: Brunner/Mazel.

Lankton, S. & Lankton, C. (1983). *The Answer Within: A Clinical Framework of Ericksonian Hypnotherapy.* New York: Brunner/Mazel.

Lankton, S., Lankton, C., & Brown, M. (1981). Psychological level communication and transactional analysis. *Transactional Analysis Journal, 11,* 287-299.

Leveton, A.F. (1982). Family therapy as play: The contribution of Milton H. Erickson, M.D. In J.K. Zeig (Ed.), *Ericksonian Approaches to Hypnosis and Psychotherapy* (pp. 201-213). New York: Brunner/Mazel.

Lustig, H.S. (1985). The enigma of Erickson's therapeutic paradoxes. In J.K. Zeig (Ed.), *Ericksonian Psychotherapy, Volume II: Clinical Applications* (pp. 244-251). New York: Brunner/Mazel.

Madanes, C. (1985). Finding a Humorous Alternative. In J.K. Zeig (Ed.), *Ericksonian Psychotherapy, Volume II: Clinical Applications* (pp. 24-43). New York: Brunner/Mazel.

Mead, M. (1977). The originality of Milton Erickson. *American Journal of Clinical Hypnosis, 20,* 4-5.

Nemetschek, P. (1982). 1201 E. Hayward: Milton H. Erickson, M.D. In J.K. Zeig (Ed.), *Ericksonian Approaches to Hypnosis and Psychotherapy* (pp. 430-443). New York: Brunner/Mazel.

Pearson, R.E. (1982). Erickson and the lonely physician. In J.K. Zeig (Ed.), *Ericksonian Approaches to Hypnosis and Psychotherapy* (pp. 422-429). New York: Brunner/Mazel.

Rodger, B.P. (1982). Ericksonian approaches in anesthesiology. In J.K. Zeig (Ed.), *Ericksonian Approaches to Hypnosis and Psychotherapy* (pp. 317-329). New York: Brunner/Mazel.

Rosen, S. (1982a). *My Voice Will Go with You: The Teaching Tales of Milton Erickson.* New York: W.W. Norton.

Rosen, S. (1982b). The values and philosophy of Milton H. Erickson. In J.K. Zeig (Ed.), *Ericksonian Approaches to Hypnosis and Psychotherapy* (pp. 462-476). New York: Brunner/Mazel.

Rossi, E. & Ryan, M. (Eds.). (1985). *Life Reframing in Hypnosis: The Seminars, Workshops, and Lectures of Milton H. Erickson (Vol. II)*. New York: Irvington.

Rossi, E., Ryan, M., & Sharp, F. (Eds.). (1983). *Healing in Hypnosis: The Seminars, Workshops, and Lectures of Milton H. Erickson (Vol. I)*. New York: Irvington.

Schoen, S. (1983). NLP: An overview, with commentaries. *The Psychotherapy Newsletter, 1,* 16-26.

Secter, I. (1982). Seminars with Erickson: The early years. In J.K. Zeig (Ed.), *Ericksonian Approaches to Hypnosis and Psychotherapy* (pp. 447-454). New York: Brunner/Mazel.

Thompson, K. (1982). The curiosity of Milton H. Erickson, M.D. In J.K. Zeig (Ed.), *Ericksonian Approaches to Hypnosis and Psychotherapy* (pp. 413-421). New York: Brunner/Mazel.

Van Dyck, R. (1982). How to use Ericksonian approaches when you are not Milton H. Erickson. In J.K. Zeig (Ed.), *Ericksonian Approaches to Hypnosis and Psychotherapy* (pp. 5-25). New York: Brunner/Mazel.

Watzlawick, P. (1982). Erickson's contribution to the interactional view of psychotherapy. In J.K. Zeig (Ed.), *Ericksonian Approaches to Hypnosis and Psychotherapy* (pp. 147-154). New York: Brunner/Mazel.

Watzlawick, P. (1985). Hypnotherapy without trance. In J.K. Zeig (Ed.), *Ericksonian Psychotherapy, Volume I: Structures* (pp. 5-14). New York: Brunner/Mazel.

Wilk, J. (1985). Ericksonian therapeutic patterns: A pattern which connects. In J.K. Zeig (Ed.), *Ericksonian Psychotherapy, Volume II: Clinical Applications* (pp. 210-233). New York: Brunner/Mazel.

Yapko, M. (1985). The Erickson hook: Values in Ericksonian approaches. In J.K. Zeig (Ed.), *Ericksonian Psychotherapy, Volume I: Structures* (pp. 266-281). New York: Brunner/Mazel.

Zeig, J.K. (1974). Hypnotherapy techniques with psychotic inpatients. *American Journal of Clinical Hypnosis, 17,* 59-69.

Zeig, J.K. (Ed.). (1980a). *A Teaching Seminar with Milton H. Erickson.* New York: Brunner/Mazel.

Zeig, J.K. (1980b). Symptom prescription and Ericksonian principles of hypnosis and psychotherapy. *American Journal of Clinical Hypnosis, 23,* 16-22.

Zeig, J.K. (1982). Ericksonian approaches to promote abstinence from cigarette smoking. *Ericksonian Approaches to Hypnosis and Psychotherapy.* New York: Brunner/Mazel.

Zeig, J.K. (1985a). The clinical use of amnesia: Ericksonian methods. In J.K. Zeig (Ed.), *Ericksonian Psychotherapy, Volume I: Structures* (pp. 317-337). New York: Brunner/Mazel.

Zeig, J.K. (Ed.). (1985b). Ethical issues in Ericksonian hypnosis: Informed consent and training standards. In Zeig (Ed.), *Ericksonian Psychotherapy, Volume I: Structures* (pp. 459-473). New York: Brunner/Mazel.

Zeig, J.K. (Ed., Introduction and Commentary). (1985c). The case of Barbie: An Ericksonian approach to the treatment of anorexia nervosa. *Transactional Analysis Journal, 15,* 85-92.